CONCEPTS OF GOVERNMENTAL AUDITING

READINGS FROM

the INTERNAL AUDITOR

Journal of The Institute of Internal Auditors

Edited by Mortimer A. Dittenhofer, PhD, CIA
The American University

Assisted by Robert B. Brown, CPA

The Institute of Internal Auditors, Inc.
International Headquarters
249 Maitland Avenue, Altamonte Springs, Florida 32701

acknowledgments

The editor and The Institute of Internal Auditors, Inc., acknowledge the assistance of the following Washington, D.C., Chapter members, selected by Rudy Arena, CIA, president of the Washington Chapter. These members served as a panel of experts in selecting the articles to be published.

Robert B. Brown, CPA, Consultant

Kenneth J. Day, CIA, General Services Administration

Ancel A. Markowitz, CIA, Martin Marietta Corporation

John T. Nockett, Washington Suburban Sanitary Commission

John L. Bastress, Montgomery County, Maryland

Warren L. Wood, CPA, Alexander Grant & Co.

William F. Wilkerson, CIA, U.S. Department of Health, Education & Welfare

Robert B. Brown, a former member of the General Accounting Office work group on audit standards, was, with the editor, an originator of the idea that culminated in this book of readings.

ISBN 0-89413-059-5

77084-Dec77

preface

In December 1975 the Governmental and Public Affairs Committee of The Institute of Internal Auditors conceived the idea of publishing a collection of the best articles that have appeared in the "Accountability Auditing in the Community" (Government) section of *The Internal Auditor.*

The collection would have a series of objectives: to serve as an operational manual for audit staffs, to contribute to the literature available for the training of auditors, to be a reference book on internal auditing in governments, and to provide a source of comparative information.

The collection, as it is constituted, contains philosophies of internal auditing — concepts, methodologies, and procedures. The authors are recognized authorities in federal, state, and local government auditing. To select those articles that would be most suitable, a panel of six judges was chosen from three governmental levels, from the CPA profession, and from academia.

Each article was judged as to the audit area most appropriate for it to be classified in and its suitability for publication. Of the 88 articles considered, 72 were selected as appropriate for this particular project. This is no reflection on the quality of the 16 not selected. Several of them were of topical interest at the time of publication. Others were not selected because they related to limited subject areas and were not of general interest.

The articles have been classified into chapters according to the categories that the panel of experts considered appropriate. Each chapter is preceded by a prefatory section. In addition, an introductory chapter contains an overview of subjects considered important to the discipline of governmental internal auditing.

The concept of the book of readings was tested by a survey that indicated significant interest on the part of college and university faculties, state audit staffs, local government audit staffs, federal audit staffs, and Certified Public Accountants. It is believed that this book is responsive to their needs.

The Institute is indebted to the writers who have given their time to provide the material for this important section of *The Internal Auditor.* The section continues to receive favorable comment from governmental auditors who read and use it. Because of their universal applicability, many of the articles are also being used by non-government audit staffs. The credit, however, belongs to the contributors.

Mortimer A. Dittenhofer

October 1977

contents

1
introduction

THE GOVERNMENTAL AUDIT

Auditing in government is not new. As a matter of fact, internal auditing received much of its impetus from government. However, the progressive type of auditing that has been synonymous with The Institute of Internal Auditors, Inc., has not been common at all levels of government.

The General Accounting Office (GAO) has practiced this type of auditing for nearly two decades. Several federal agencies, including the Energy Research and Development Agency (formerly the Atomic Energy Commission) and the National Aeronautics and Space Administration (NASA), have engaged in audit operations exceeding the traditional financial examination.

Progress has been made in state auditing during the last ten years, beginning in Michigan and California. Progress in local governments has not been as notable. Some larger cities and counties are extending audits beyond financial and compliance areas.

The basic drive behind this evolutionary movement has been a change in the concepts of governmental accountability. There is a need for more information about the management of governmental entities. This information is needed by various government echelons and is being increasingly sought by the public, public-interest groups, and the media.

Thus, no longer are public officials required to be accountable only for honesty, for fidelity in the handling of governmental resources. They must be equally accountable for handling these resources as efficiently and effectively as practical.

The concept of visibility has caused another change in attitude toward governmental management and, concurrently, auditing. The public and its surrogate, the media, are no longer willing to accept governmental management *carte blanche*. The back-room slogan "We're doing it in your best interests; trust us" is no longer acceptable. The public is interested in *what* is being done, *why* it is necessary, and *how* it will be accomplished. Thus, the release of audit reports to the public is a current issue. It has a multitude of behavioral implications.

Another factor that has encouraged internal auditing is the size and complexity of today's government processes. The auditor must assist the manager in reviewing and evaluating the management processes. The auditor acts as an independent observer in providing technical expertise for on-site review of government functions. This aspect of auditing is essentially management-oriented and concerns itself with efficiency, economy, and effectiveness in governmental operations. Because the auditor is a specialist in managerial controls, some of the technical expertise must be obtained from consultants or from specialists on the audit staff.

Elmer B. Staats, comptroller general of the United States, reported three important changes in governmental auditing during the last ten years. These changes are:

1. Audits aimed at improving economy and efficiency of operations have become commonplace and are practiced at all levels of government.

2. Auditing has become more difficult — even financial audits — because the computer has become a common accounting tool. Because of its complexity, auditors have had to acquire considerable specialized knowledge.

3. The most dramatic change, however, is the emergence of the program-results audit.

Accountability in Government

All governments and all officials of government are accountable for the resources with which they have been supplied to accomplish specific objectives. Financial reports and operating reports assist in discharging this accountability. The operational auditor is a part of this discharge mechanism in two ways: first, by lending credibility to these statements and, second, by providing information for interested managers and outsiders as to the efficiency and effectiveness with which governments and officials have employed their resources.

Resources include money, materials, manpower, equipment, facilities, and time. All these can be measured with regard to input into government operations. However, output in many governmental areas is not measured as easily. In education, public health, and public welfare, the intrinsic value of improvements of operations or the alleviation of undesirable conditions is not easy to quantify in dollars, although much of the output can be identified as to quantitative data.

The concept of accountability has social and psychological connotations. One of the basic tenets is that the use of resources implies a need for them in society.

The Standards of Auditing Today

Every profession, to be worthy of the name, must have standards. These standards may serve several purposes. One result of the use of standards is to insure that work performed is of high quality. Other benefits include providing a means of internal quality control and supplying the criteria to be used by an external audit organization to determine the acceptability of audits performed by others.

Standards for financial auditing were developed and are being used by the American Institute of Certified Public Accountants (AICPA). These standards, first issued in codified form in 1968 and then reissued as *Statements on Auditing Standards* in 1973, apply exclusively to financial audits performed by CPA's. They are still in the process of development and new statements are continually being issued.

Government auditors who, in many organizations, were expanding the parameters of the audit beyond the traditional financial aspects, felt the need for more extensive standards than those of the AICPA.

In 1969, Comptroller General Staats convened a work group of federal, state, and local audit specialists who, together with academicians and members of the AICPA and IIA as well as members of other professional associations, developed a set of standards that would be appropriate for the full-scope audits being conducted by some progressive governmental audit organizations.

These *Standards for Audit of Governmental Organizations, Programs, Activities, and Functions* were issued in 1972 and revised slightly in 1974. No interpretations or extensions of the standards have been issued, although the GAO has issued a series of supplemental booklets aimed at assisting in the implementation of the standards.

The standards have had a favorable influence on many audit staffs and much of the progress made in auditing during the past five years can be attributed to their use.

However, adhering to the standards imposes some constraints on auditing. For instance, such audits require more time. Also, the cost of audits increases because a staff with greater skills is needed. In addition, there is less acceptability because of the newness of some of the audit concepts. And there is a constant need for updating because of the dynamic characteristics of the processes included in the audits.

Yet, the advantages far surpass the disadvantages. The most important benefit is improved management of governments. The greater visibility of the activities of public officials is also a much needed, new development. The public accounting profession has confirmed its support of the standards. Thus, the standards may prove to be one of the most profound influences on government management in recent times.

What Is Performance Auditing?

This term is frequently used to identify an auditing process otherwise known as operational auditing, functional auditing, management auditing, program review, internal audit, and internal review. Some writers choose to provide separate definitions for each, thus differentiating one from another. The Institute of Internal Auditors provided an extensive treatment of the semantics of performance auditing in its *Research Report No. 19*, published in 1975.

Performance and operational auditing are optional names for the same process but are differentiated from the other types of auditing by the extent of coverage. Performance auditing is an extension of the audit beyond, but including, financial and compliance aspects. In this regard, performance and operational auditing include the audit of the economy and efficiency with which an auditee is managing resources as well as the audit of the degree to which management is achieving program results.

It is recognized that not all audits will entail the full-scope audit described above. Specific areas can be identified for audit based on the type of operation being audited, the resources available, or the belief that the potential benefits from a full-scope audit would not favorably compare with the cost of the audit.

Because of the breadth of coverage of the full-scope performance audit, processes are used that are supplementary to the usual auditing of financial operations. The survey approach, emphasizing interviews and physical inspections, becomes very important, and the use of operations research or program analysis is a part of many complex audit engagements. Skills in management, sociology, economics, statistics, and public administration are frequently needed.

There are more behavioral aspects because the auditors are working in an area where subjective determinations become part of the audit process. Also, auditors often review the performances of executives and groups of workers. At times, competence and judgment issues are the substance of the audit. Interpersonal relations assume greater importance in achieving cooperation during the audit and in obtaining a commitment on the part of the auditee to correct conditions disclosed by the audit. Candor and honesty in conferences, timely and full disclosure of findings as they are disclosed, and a constructive tone in audit reports are essential to an effective audit.

The Operational Auditor: Reporter or Staff

Governmental auditors serve in varying capacities. They are generally considered to be internal auditors — that is, internal to a unit of government. Thus, auditors of a particular local government, auditing parts of that government relative to state or federal interests, are internal auditors. However, when they, as central governmental auditors, audit a department or branch of that government, they are external to that department or branch. Then auditors operate in different capacities.

As external auditors, governmental auditors act as evaluators and reporters of those activities within the purview of the auditee. They may conduct audits of any scope desired: financial/compliance, efficiency, or effectiveness. They are objective in their reviews of auditee operations and prepare reports of their findings for the local legislative body and for its top management. At times their examinations disclose improper practices that appear to be caused by malfunction of the auditee's staff or organizational structure. However, further investigation may identify the basic cause to be a failure much closer to home.

An example might be improper procurement actions caused by procurement personnel who were not well informed. The underlying cause might well have been a poor communication policy in the comptroller's shop. In this case, auditors are, if they report to the comptroller, faced with the responsibility of being both reporters and staff — reporters in disclosing the improper procurement handling and staff in identifying the basic cause as a failure in the office to which they report.

Auditors serve as staff when they perform audit functions within their own organizational unit. They also can serve as audit advisors to their supervisors relative to internal audit staffs common to lower echelon units, or external auditors of high echelons. In the cases of lower-level audit staffs, they may conduct quality control reviews of their operations, either as a specific audit function to assure that they are operating efficiently or on an ad hoc basis to determine the degree of reliance that can be placed on lower echelon audits in areas where they also have an audit responsibility.

Auditors can serve as staff by assisting in the design of internal control methods and in establishing policy relative to coordination with audit staffs of the federal government, with other local governments, or with the audit staffs of subordinate units. This staff capacity also includes the performance of special studies of an audit nature made for the unit's legislative arm and for the unit's top management.

Independence

Independence and its presumption is one of the important auditing standards and a necessary ingredient for operational or performance audits. Independence allows auditors freedom to audit as they believe necessary and to report objectively the results of their auditing. Independence involves the auditor's personal state of mind, freedom from interference in conduct of the audit, and organizational placement so as to be free from sanctions and influence.

Governmental auditors must be free from pressures caused by their own convictions, attitudes, or background. There also must be freedom from pressures caused by actions of the auditee. There must be freedom from activities of peer groups whose operations could be affected by the outcome of the audit. Finally, there must be freedom from influence of client organizations whose reputation, status, or operations could be impacted by audit findings.

Proper organizational placement of the audit operation can do much to guarantee independence. In the private sector, auditors are most frequently free from constraints when reporting to the Audit Committee of the Board of Directors. In the public sector, the trend is toward a similar committee of the legislative branch.

Achieving independence is not an easy task. In governments auditors are either elected by a constituency, appointed by an executive branch official with or without approval of a legislative unit, or elected or appointed by the legislature. Therefore, auditors are either elected executives or employees. Thus, in addition to normal employer-employee relationships there are also political pressures that can constrain objective auditing and reporting.

Auditors faced with disclosing information that will discredit their political party or the party currently in control are in a dilemma. Their honest reporting could cause problems for the party and possibly for them in the next election. Long terms of office with freedom from sanctions will frequently insure a state of mind conducive to objective examination, evaluation, and reporting.

Auditors are independent checks on management. They must have no ties to that management from personal involvement, either past or present. In government, where there are also moral, political, social, or economic issues that impact on the decision-making process of management, auditors must walk a tightrope to insure that reporting is not clouded by personal attitudes or convictions. Finally, auditors must remain intellectually honest in determining the appropriateness and propriety of actions and decisions of the auditee.

Auditors must be perceived by others, including the media, as truly independent. This requirement precludes words or actions that could mar this perception and destroy belief in their impartiality and candor.

2
accountability

It is appropriate that this subject introduce the readings of *Auditing in Government.* Accountability is the basis of government operations. It requires governmental units or officials to report to those providing resources as to how these resources have been used. It is accountability that influences constituencies and others to make resources available.

Unfortunately, accountability is not always understood. Sometimes it is ignored. At times the reporting system is deficient or does not operate properly. Thus, the responsibility to report is not carried out. Sometimes reporting is not accurate or is not responsive to requirements established by those to whom information should be provided. A means to correct these conditions and to disclose the reason for their existence is needed. Where there has been no reporting, surrogate reporting is needed. Thus, the auditor.

Accountability is especially important in government. It is important because of the absence of the profit concept, the economic balancing in the private sector that automatically establishes for stockholders and others a reporting system that discloses the efficiency and effectiveness of operations. Also, the output of business is goods and services. Both of these can be measured.

Government has no profit concept and its output of services is not measurable in many cases. Also, governments do not have the same attitude as business toward the impact of inefficiency, diseconomy, and unfaithfulness of the ordinary citizen. Some means must be devised to supplement the traditional governmental reporting system which is accountability-oriented only in budgetary matters. Internal auditing in government is one means. It provides the information needed to evaluate how well organizations and officials handle resources entrusted to them.

In some cases, there will be control systems that monitor efficiency and effectiveness. Here, auditors determine the validity of results reported by managements. When there are no systems, auditors must make such studies, reviews, and evaluations as well as report on the efficiency and effectiveness of the operations.

The four articles in this section describe accountability in governments in more detail. The first article, by the editor, discusses accountability as a concept. The second article, by Dr. Robert J. Freeman, takes another view and explains the internal auditor's accountability to the public. Then, Audit Director Harold Sellers, U.S.

Department of Transportation, describes accountability in federal agencies and tells how the auditor can be responsive to the demands of accountability. In the fourth article, Wisconsin State Auditor Robert R. Ringwood discusses the accountability of state auditing to state legislatures and their constituencies.

Accountability in Government

Dr. Mortimer A. Dittenhofer, CIA

The Internal Auditor Sept./Oct. 1974

Accountability is a characteristic or a function so frequently taken for granted that there is an absence of literature on the subject. Comment can be found as parts of works that deal with other subjects but there are few books or articles that deal expressly with the subject.

Accountability and audit are so inextricably wound together that without one there generally cannot be the other. Audit normally is not effective unless someone or some organization is accountable for resources of some sort. On the other hand, accountability cannot be fully discharged without an affirmation that the reports of the discharge of accountability are credible.

It is because of this proximity that we, as auditors, have such a great interest in the subject. Even then, the references in auditing texts are infrequent; and many auditors are unaware of the psychological, moral, political and economic forces that may constrain managers to ignore the issues of accountability or to operate inefficiently or uneconomically. These disincentives will be our main element of discussion.

Accountability is as important in government as it is in industry. Today's government official is provided with many resources with which to carry out his assigned duties and achieve his delegated objectives. He is accountable for his use of them in these endeavors as is today's industrial executive. Although government – except for various types of enterprise operations such as public utilities, prison industries, toll roads and bridges, and other similar operations — does not operate on a profit basis or even on a full-cost recovery basis, the official is using valuable resources and is accountable for their use.

What is Accountability?

What then is this function of accountability? In 1951 Ralph Davis, a student of and writer on management, identified it as "a requirement or condition under which each member of the organization renders a report on his discharge of responsibilities and is judged fairly on the basis of his record of accomplishment."[1]

Davis, as well as other writers dealing with the subject, holds that a prerequisite for accountability is the specification of performance standards by which the accomplishments can be judged. This is frequently a problem in governments, for such standards in terms of quantity, quality, time or cost are frequently missing.

Accountability in governments applies to all of the governmental branches: executive, legislative and judicial, since all have resources with which to work. As a matter of fact, many elected governmental auditors of state and local governments consider themselves a fourth branch in the separation of powers context. They say that they act as the surrogate of the public, the evaluator, to determine how well this accountability has been accomplished by the other branches. Thus, legislatures and local councils are accountable for the results accomplished by organizations operating under their direction and overview. The officials of such governments are accountable to successively higher echelons for their assigned resources.

To establish accountability, governments and constituencies, through their legislators, state their objectives, aims and expectations in laws, regulations, constitutions, charters, budgets and other expressions of public policy. The activities and accomplishments of all levels of government are then evaluated against these objectives, expectations and performance standards. And the governmental unit or official is expected to be answerable. The organization is expected to be frank, candid and informative, its "cards on the table, its life an open book."[2]

In a democratic society, governments are usually accountable for what they do or do not do, "how and how well they do it, the results they achieve or fail to bring about, the good or bad judgment they display in adopting and carrying out public policies, their custody and disposition of public resources and other large and small matters."[3] Accountability then descends or extends: each succeeding lower or horizontal level holding those accountable to whom it has supplied resources. These resources may have been assigned informally through normal government operations, or they could be provided formally through agreements, budgets, contracts and grants. The important element is the assignment by one level and the acceptance and use by another element of the government.

The Discharge of Accountability

Accountability traditionally has been considered as providing a formal statement of money transactions and the condition, financially speaking, of an organization or a program. A more comprehensive definition would be to give reasons for and explanations of what one does.

A financial statement will rarely perform this added function. It can,

---

[1]Ralph C. Davis, *The Fundamentals of Top Management* (New York: Harper & Row, 1951), p. 320.

[2]The Comptroller General of the United States, *Auditors Agents for Good Government* (Washington, D.C.: Government Printing Office, 1973), p. 2.

[3]*Ibid.*

on occasion, "hide more than it reveals."[4] Thus, there is a need for what might be called "public accountability," what Normanton describes as an "obligation to provide for independent and impartial observers holding the right of reporting their findings at the highest levels in the state, any available information about financial information which they may request."[5] "The state auditor acts on behalf of a public power . . . whether that power be an individual, a group, an assembly or an abstraction called 'the people.' "[6]

Just in passing, this concept of public accountability is not a newcomer to the government scene. We have evidence of the practice in classical Athens, through the absolute monarchies of the Renaissance where the servant rendered an accounting to the monarch's auditors, to the constitutional states of the twentieth century when the concept of separation of powers came into more universal use and where the "managing power became itself accountable to the power which made the law in matters of receipt and expenditure."[7] For such accountability to become a realistic process in today's complex governmental operation, it demands a structure of planning, control and feedback techniques with a sophistication of organization, policy and practice for each.

---

[4]E. L. Normanton, *Accountability and Audit in Government* (New York: Praeger Press, 1966), p. 1.

[5]*Ibid.*, p. 2.

[6]*Ibid.*

[7]*Ibid.*, p. 4.

The Governmental Internal Auditor's Accountability to the Public

Dr. Robert J. Freeman, CPA

The Internal Auditor Nov./Dec. 1974

"Accountability" or "being accountable" may be defined as "having to report, explain or justify one's actions or inactions; being answerable for one's performance to another person or group." If one is accountable, as defined, there are two related questions: To whom? For what? These must be answered in order to make the concept operational.

The issue of concern here is: *What accountability, if any, does the government internal auditor have to the public?* One's initial response may well be "none," and there is considerable support for this position.

The Statement of Responsibilities of the Internal Auditor issued by The Institute of Internal Auditors (IIA) states that internal auditing is "a service to management." It is designed "to assist all members of management in the effective discharge of *their* responsibilities." The internal auditor's principal responsibility is "to inform and advise management."[1] Although a section of that *Statement* deals with "independence," it is concerned with the need for the internal auditor to be objective and to have independence *within* the organization (internal independence) in order to serve top management effectively, not with the independence *from* top management (external independence) required of the external auditor.[2]

This emphasis is borne out in the *IIA Code of Ethics.* The preamble of that *Code* states that "managements rely on . . . internal auditing to assist in the fulfillment of *their management stewardship.*" Article II reads in part: "A member, in holding the trust of his employer, shall exhibit loyalty in all matters pertaining to the affairs of the employer."[3] Furthermore, as indicated by the subtitle, the "service-to-management" theme permeates Lawrence B. Sawyer's milestone book in this field, *The Practice of Modern Internal Auditing: Appraising Operations for Management.*[4] Still further, in his instant classic, *The Accountability and Audit of Governments,* E. L. Normanton acknowledges (or asserts) that internal audit in government, as in private business, is "a confidential service to the administrative and political heads of departments."[5]

"Accountable" and "Accountability" in Theory and Practice

Thus, if we limit usage of the terms "accountable" and "accountability" to those aspects of one's performance responsibility for which he is *formally* and *directly* accountable and on which he must report regularly, as is commonly done, and if we agree that the government internal auditor is an employee of agency management rather than part of that management, then we may safely conclude that the governmental internal auditor is *not* accountable to the public (externally) but only to his employer management (internally). This is the prevailing view of contemporary theory and practice.

If we view the government internal auditor as a member of the agency management team rather than merely an employee of management and as a member of a profession for which ethical and other performance standards have been established, a different perspective begins to emerge. If we take cognizance of the rapidly evolving intergovernmental audit network in-

---

[1]"Statement of Responsibilities of the Internal Auditor," The Institute of Internal Auditors, Inc., is reprinted as Appendix G, pp. 513-514 of *The Practice of Modern Internal Auditing* by Lawrence B. Sawyer.

[2]Ibid.

[3]"Code of Ethics," The Institute of Internal Auditors, Inc., is reprinted as Appendix H, pp. 515-516 of *The Practice of Modern Internal Auditing* by Lawrence B. Sawyer.

[4]Lawrence B. Sawyer, *The Practice of Modern Internal Auditing: Appraising Operations for Management* (Orlando, Florida: The Institute of Internal Auditors, Inc., 1973).

[5]E. L. Normanton, *The Accountability and Audit of Governments: A Comparative Study* (New York, New York: Fredrick A. Praeger, Inc., Publishers, 1966), p. 23.

terdependencies and responsibilities and include within the purview of "accountability" those responsibilities one has for which he *may* be held accountable either now or in the near future, it becomes apparent that the governmental internal auditor is indeed accountable to the public as well as to external auditors and to his profession.

For what aspects of his performance is he now accountable in this broader sense? For what aspects may he be held formally accountable in the not-too-distant future?

Since he is a member of the internal auditing profession, the public – together with external auditors and the internal auditing profession – may properly expect a professional level of competence and performance. The *minimum standards* for performance evaluation would seem to be those set forth in the *IIA Statement of Responsibilities of the Internal Auditor* and *Code of Ethics* together with those in *Standards for Audit of Governmental Organizations, Programs, Activities & Functions.*[6] Beyond these are the common law and common expectations that a professional person will continually strive to perform to his potential, to upgrade his capabilities through a lifelong program of formal and informal continuing education, and to stay abreast of new developments in his field of expertise.

Furthermore, as Normanton observed: "Executive accountability can be considered as a matter of collective responsibility or as the sum of the responsibilities of individuals."[7] Thus, as a member of the management team, the government internal auditor is also accountable to the public directly – and through its legislative representatives – for his actions or inactions to attain the maximum practicable levels of agency economy, efficiency, and effectiveness. And, as a citizen-taxpayer employee, might he expect anything less of himself?

---

[6]The Comptroller General of the United States, *Standards for Audit of Governmental Organizations, Programs, Activities & Functions* (Washington, D. C.: USGPO, 1972).

[7]Normanton, op. cit., p. 81.

Accountability in the Executive Agencies

Harold Sellers

The Internal Auditor Nov./Dec. 1974

In government, there is perhaps no greater responsibility than the accountability for public resources entrusted to its elected, appointed, and career officials. The concept of accountability is fundamental to our institutions. Governmental agencies and their officials, as custodians of public resources, are accountable to the people. Accountability, therefore, requires an understanding of the functional relationship between these officials and the public.

Enactment of Applicable Laws

From time to time, laws have been and are being enacted to recognize and prescribe specific actions for satisfying public trust.

G. W. Lafferty, commenting on the influence of the law, observed that there is no phase of financial activity which, in some manner or other, is not controlled and directed by the law. The law determines the manner in which funds received are to be allocated to specific activities for expenditures and, through formally approved budgets, the purposes for which funds may be spent.[1]

The Budget and Accounting Act of 1950, as amended, requires the head of each federal agency to establish and maintain systems of accounting and internal control designed to provide: (1) full disclosure of the financial results of the agency's activities and (2) effective control and accountability for all funds, property, and other assets for which the agency is responsible. Procedures for certifying and disbursing officers in the authorization and disbursement of federal funds are prescribed in 31 USC 82.

Other laws bear on the accountability for government property. The National Security Act (10 USC 2701) includes provisions for the Secretary of Defense to maintain property records on both quantitative and monetary bases. Public Law 84-863 [31 USC 66a (c)] provides for the accounting system of each agency to include adequate monetary property accounting records. The Federal Property and Administrative Services Act of 1949 [40 USC 483b] requires each executive agency to maintain adequate inventory controls and accountability systems for property under its control.

The foregoing demonstrates the emphasis placed on establishing and maintaining controls as an essential function in the accountability process.

Monitoring Functions of Certain Agencies

To assure effective compliance with the laws, certain federal agencies and offices have been assigned specific responsibilities. The Treasury Department maintains a system of central accounting for the purpose of providing financial reports for the federal government. This centralized accounting reflects financial information furnished by other federal agencies and those financial transactions entered into directly by the Treasury Department.

The Office of Management and Budget monitors and directs diverse aspects of the financial and budgetary affairs of all federal agencies in connection with the preparation and execution of the budget.

The General Services Administration prescribes policies and procedures to be followed in procurement, supply and property acquisition and retention activities in each federal agency.

[1]G. W. Lafferty, "Influence of the Law on the Independent Accountant in the Examination of Local Government Accounts," *Journal of Accountancy* (New York, New York: August 1950).

Charting the Accountability Process

Accountability in executive agencies may be said to originate with the preparation of the annual budget. It is during this process that consideration is given initially to all areas of resource acquisition and disposal. Approval of the budget and appropriation of funds by the Congress set in motion the events contemplated in the budget process.

Release of funds is controlled by the Office of Management and Budget through the issuance of quarterly apportionments of appropriations which indicate the amounts of funds available for obligation during the period and for the respective authorized purposes.

Quantitative restraints are also imposed on federal agencies by the Congress in matters such as personnel hiring and acquisition of real and personal property.

Adherence to quantity limitations on personnel and capital items are monitored by the Office of Management and Budget, and periodic reporting by agencies has been instituted in this process.

Benefits of Control Systems

The presence of laws, however, should not be construed as primary justification for instituting control systems. While laws serve to prescribe certain measures to which elected, appointed, and career officials must conform, there are other compelling reasons why such controls should be applied.

Moore and Stettler recall the unknown sage who observed that business runs on paper tracks. These tracks are the accounting system: the paperwork and procedures from which data are gathered and processed to provide information needed by management to control the business enterprise.[2]

The business of government is no less dependent on adequate systems as a major factor needed by its officials to exercise similar control.

A major function of the accounting system as a management control technique is to provide feedback through which levels of management may ascertain the results of applying overall policies and making day-to-day operating decisions, thereby acquiring further basis for reaching new decisions concerning future actions.[3]

Feedback is provided primarily through various reports and statements prepared from data processed through the accounting system and supplemented by such techniques as budgeting and criteria for appraising program results.

Another type of control found useful to management is internal control. This control is essentially an automatic or self-regulating system designed to assure management that all safeguards are operating effectively. The Committee on Auditing Procedure of the American Institute of Certified Public Accountants has defined internal control as "comprising the plan of organization and all of the coordinate methods and measures adopted within a business to safeguard its assets, check the accuracy and reliability of its accounting data, provide operational efficiency and en-

---

[2]Francis E. Moore and Howard F. Stettler, *Accounting Systems for Management Control* (Homewood, Illinois: Richard D. Irwin, 1963).

[3]Ibid.

courage adherence to prescribed managerial policies."[4]

Included among the methods and measures are such items as independent accountability, proofs and controls, manuals of procedures, and internal audits.

The need for internal audits is demonstrated as agency officials strive to ascertain:

(1) whether policies, lines or authority and procedures are actually being observed in daily operations;

(2) the soundness and adequacy of accounting and other controls;

(3) assets are being properly accounted for; and

(4) quality of performance in carrying out assigned responsibilities.

Internal audit fulfills this need by continuous review and appraisal of these activities and by providing recommendations for improvements or assurances of their adequate functioning or notifications of violations of laws and regulations.

Accountability in executive agencies is a comprehensive process. It is aided by the conviction that management controls contribute to the successful discharge of the public trust but do not replace human awareness.

[4]Committee on Auditing Procedures, *Internal Control – Special Report* (New York, New York: the American Institute of Certified Public Accountants, 1949).

Accountability to the State Legislature

Robert R. Ringwood, CIA, CPA

The Internal Auditor Nov./Dec. 1974

One of the basic areas of accountability that any employee owes his employer is to perform in such a way so that he assists his employer in carrying out his accountabilities. Thus, before we determine what the legislative auditor's responsibilities are to the state legislature, we should discuss the state legislature's areas of accountability.

Among the many accountability areas of the state legislature, there are two areas of accountability to the public, where the legislative auditor may be of assistance:

- In the area of legislation, the primary function of legislatures, the individual legislators would like to know the results of present ongoing programs and the efficiency of their operation.
- Another area of concern to state legislators is legislative

overview. To perform ably in this area, each legislator would like to be informed not only about program results but on how well program administrators are accounting for assets entrusted to their care: Did management devise plans? Do they have control? Do they have adequate feedback and a means for self-evaluation? Have they considered alternative methods to accomplish their aims more economically, etc.?

Legislative Auditor Performs in All Audit Elements

It becomes apparent that the legislative auditor is not only accountable to furnish financial information to the legislature but that he must evaluate management's organizational framework, their controls, their communication systems (both the formal and the informal ones), management's planning systems, and management information systems. Has management set goals and objectives for the program? Have they established measurement criteria? Do they have a system for comparing actual results against the plan? In short, the legislative auditor, in order to carry out his accountabilities to the legislature, must perform in all three elements of governmental auditing:

- Financial and compliance
- Efficiency and economy
- Program results

The legislative auditor is not only accountable to furnish the data to the legislature but is also accountable to provide it in nontechnical language, as concisely as clarity will allow, and in a timely manner. To provide needed data in a timely manner, the legislative auditor must devise methods to determine what the legislature's current concerns are. Better yet, the auditor should find a way to determine what the legislature's interests will be during the next session. No legislative auditor has a perfect method in getting the right data to the legislature at the right time. We must all improve in this aspect. Some methods that have worked are using legislative audit committees, auditors attending the standing-committees' meetings, listening with an open mind to the needs of individual legislators, etc.

Setting Priorities

In order to be successful in fulfilling his accountability, the legislative auditor must always have the concerns of the legislature as his highest priority in scheduling audits. Other priorities such as program size, program vulnerability, program sensitivity, and statutory obligations become secondary. He is accountable to the legislators to inform them about these secondary priorities; however, in the final analysis, determining program priorities is the responsibility of the legislature. Thus, the legislative auditor should always consider the concerns of the legislature first in scheduling audits.

The legislative auditor is accountable to furnish his data from a bipartisan viewpoint, to avoid personal bias, to be objective, and to perform in a professional manner. To accomplish this, he must establish adequate training programs for his staff. He must also establish objectives for his audit and should always be aware that his first responsibility is to the legislature. He must remember that the legislature is responsible to the people, who want factual information. The legislative auditor must not attempt to put unfavorable facts in storage. The public is demanding that the data their governments give them be true, complete, and unbiased. Therefore, the greatest area of accountability of the legislative auditor to the legislature is to give the legislature the truth as it exists and not what they would prefer to hear. The legislative auditor should never be guilty of holding back data because he fears it is not what his bosses would like. If that happens, he is not being accountable to the legislature, to the public, or even to himself.

3
development of audit standards

Standards are criteria for evaluation. Auditors in public practice have used standards for many years to guide their activities. These standards, issued by the AICPA, have had a profound effect on all auditors in government and industry.

In 1969, Comptroller General of the U.S., Elmer B. Staats, determined that standards were needed for governmental auditing. He convened a work group of federal, state, and local auditors who worked with members of academia, the AICPA, IIA and other professional organizations. Together, they developed a set of standards to meet the needs of auditors performing full-scope audits in progressive governmental audit organizations. The result was the issuance of *Standards for Audit of Governmental Organizations, Programs, Activities, and Functions* in 1972. A slight revision was made to the standards in 1974.

The impact of the GAO standards has been quite profound not only on government auditors but on public accountants and on internal auditors in business and industry. Many CPA firms have conducted classes on the standards for their members.

Also, The Institute of Internal Auditors has issued an exposure draft of five internal auditing standards covering independence, professional proficiency, scope of work, performance of audit work, and management of the internal audit function. These standards cover the general area of practice. Other standards are forthcoming on the areas of conduct, including ethics, qualifications, and professional relations.

Although the AICPA has not officially endorsed the GAO standards, one of its authoritative publications does identify them as providing for a type of auditing that practitioners should consider. This is a sign of the times.

The GAO standards have not been widely recognized in professional literature, although texts on governmental accounting and auditing are beginning to discuss them. The subject of audit standards is frequently covered in seminar programs. State and local government audit manuals are increasingly mentioning them specifically or by reference. Shortly after the standards were issued, the Office of Management and Budget made them mandatory for federal audit activities.

Adherence to the GAO standards results in auditing which is responsive to the increasing demand for new and better public service.

Since one of the objectives of this auditing is improved management, the public benefits from it. This type of auditing is also more responsive to the evaluation of the accountability of efficient and effective use of public resources by public servants. Many of the advances in public administration have resulted from the principal characteristics of this progressive type of auditing: the expansion of audit effort into areas of management (efficiency and economy) and program results (effectiveness).

A number of benefits will accrue to the auditing discipline as well as to society as a result of these standards. In summary they will:

- Improve the quality of auditing in government by providing goals
- Serve as criteria that can be used by other auditors in determining the reliance they can place on audit organizations
- Help make better evaluations of government operations for the purpose of accountability determination and management assistance
- Tend to stimulate the discipline to self-improvement
- Help reduce duplicate auditing by improving original audit operations
- Serve as a guide for audit training and education

The articles included in this section treat various aspects of audit standards. The first article, "Internal Auditing Goes Public Under the 'Standard'" by Professor Jimmy D. Stewart, treats some of the basic concepts on which the standards were developed. Dr. Gerald D. Brighton continues with comments on the concepts and development efforts in "Developing Audit Standards to Evaluate Outputs." He is critical of academia for its neglect of internal auditing, both in teaching and research.

Frederic A. Heim, Jr., describes the use of audit standards as a basis for federal audit guides. He identifies a series of requirements that can serve audit organizations needing to modernize their audit guides.

Two prominent, local government auditors, Lloyd F. Hara of King County, Seattle, Washington, and Daniel Paul of Baltimore, discuss the application of the standards to municipal operations. Hara describes the impact of standards on training and the quality of local government output. He also discusses factors that made improved auditing so welcome. Paul emphasizes independence, possibly the most important standard. He relates this standard to the pronouncements of the National Committee on Governmental Accounting.

The section concludes with a case study on independence. Harvey M. Rose, who recently served as auditor general of California, presents his side of an experience which constrained his independence in auditing. This controversial case brings to issue some basic concepts of the independence standard. The article vividly describes how one individual sees the potential problems related to independence. This is an area where cases are difficult to obtain.

Internal Auditing Goes Public Under the 'Standard'

Jimmy D. Stewart

The Internal Auditor Jan./Feb. 1973

The intergovernmental transfer of public funds from the federal government to state and local governments, and the intrastate allocation and reallocation of the funds provided under a myriad of grant-in-aid programs, has created a demand for effective independent accountability reviews and attendant public reports by post-auditors representing all levels of government. Such reviews of the accountability of public officials include not only evaluations of fiscal integrity and compliance with applicable laws and regulations (fiscal accountability), but also evaluations of operational economy and efficiency (managerial accountability) and evaluations of the degree of fulfillment of mandated program objectives and the efficiency, i.e., selection of alternative approaches on a least cost basis, with which these objectives are fulfilled (program accountability).

It is obvious that such broad-gauge accountability evaluations cannot be accomplished nor can managerial or program accountability reports be rendered to the public and others if the scope of governmental audits is restricted, through an arbitrarily drawn distinction between accounting and administrative internal control, to considerations of direct financial operations and transactions. Indeed, the *Standards for Audit of Governmental Organizations, Programs, Activities and Functions* recently issued by the comptroller general of the United States envisions that, "an audit that would include provision for the interests of all potential users of governmental audits would ordinarily include provision for auditing all the above elements of the accountability of the responsible officials." The internal auditor has not previously attempted to draw this nice distinction between accounting and administrative controls, therefore, it is his audit and reporting approach which has established the pattern for audits in the public sector.

It is equally obvious that incorporating into reviews the expanded audit scope envisioned by the "Standards" will require: (1) a substantial revision of current audit techniques and procedures as well as reporting formats; (2) a greater reliance upon the evaluation of the entity's system of financial and operational control; and (3) an effective scheme for coordinating the efforts of post-auditors, governmental and private, representing the various levels of government in order to avoid duplication of effort and the inefficient use of audit resources.

A number of interested groups and individuals are actively involved in evaluating the impact of the "Standards" upon the first requirement listed. The extensive experience of Institute members with expanded-scope audits should prove invaluable in this effort. The latter two requirements, however, deserve at least equal consideration by the profession.

A sound system of comprehensive internal control within organizations, both public and private, has long been recognized as a necessity for effective managerial performance. Internal control, in a well-designed information and control system, acts as a medium through which actual financial and operating performance information can be evaluated against previously established formal or informal criteria, and the comparative results transmitted to program managers at the requisite levels within the organization for necessary corrective action. In the public sector, internal control is, therefore, an integral part of any executive department's management control system and should be subjected to critical evaluation by post-auditors representing all levels of government interested in the particular program or activity.

All financial and operational control systems require a feedback mechanism through which the effectiveness of the established controls themselves are periodically analyzed, evaluated, and reported upon by an independent appraiser. Such an evaluation must, by its very nature, be an after-the-fact performance review. The accomplishment of this control evaluation is the historical function served by qualified independent internal auditors acting in the capacity of a post-auditor.

Here is a potential danger area in the development of audit organizational structures, particularly at local governmental levels, as greater reliance upon internal control systems is required. Traditionally, the internal auditor has been viewed as an in-house executive department employee reporting only to management. Undoubtedly, the tendency will be to perpetuate this tradition. However, the internal audit function, as any other governmental function or activity, must be justified in terms of a favorable cost-benefit relationship. The rigid specification for an "internal" auditor, meaning positioned within and reporting only to the executive department of the particular governmental body, may be far too restrictive and may under particular circumstances result in requirements that are far too costly in terms of the potential benefits. While such internal positioning may, when justified by favorable cost/benefit relationships, be established within the executive department of local governments, the required control evaluation may be equally well accomplished by private contract auditors, governmental auditors functioning as a part of the legislative branch, or by auditors, private or governmental, representing interested governmental units at another level of government. The interplay of cost/benefit relationships should dictate the exact positioning of the comprehensive internal control evaluator in any given circumstance.

Developing Audit Standards To Evaluate Outputs

Gerald D. Brighton, CPA

The Internal Auditor July/Aug. 1973

In developing standards for internal auditing in general and governmental internal auditing in particular, it seems reasonable for internal auditors to look to the CPA and the academic professions for assistance. If so, internal auditors will need to continue to take the initiative.

CPAs and Academicians Focus on Input

Professional literature – the most authoritative being that of the American Institute of CPAs – academic auditing textbooks, research and courses focus on the "input" side of auditing. By input is meant the revenues received, assets and equities accounted for, and expenditures for services rendered. Audit of these inputs would commonly be labeled financial audit.

Generally, the work of a competent internal auditor is considerably broader than financial audits. He attempts to audit "outputs," that is to evaluate effectiveness of programs and services. This broader audit is called comprehensive audit or performance - operational management audit. With few exceptions, the CPA profession is seldom involved in such audits.

Report of the Committee on Auditing for Federal Agencies

One such exception is the work of the American Institute's Committee on Auditing for Federal Agencies. The Committee has issued a report addressed to "fiscal and compliance auditing" of federal grants.[1] It has promised "the issuance of additional reports which will deal with other aspects of auditing federal grants including the evolving subject of performance auditing."[2] However, the present state of the CPA's art is well summarized by that committee's comment about the scope of the external auditors' services: "Generally, however, the CPA should not be called upon to provide subjective evaluations of the technical aspects of program effectiveness and similar matters as part of the normal financial audit."[3]

The key expression is "subjective evaluations." The CPA profession has not as yet developed standards and/or procedures beyond those required for the financial audit. Subjectivity is largely a function of the lack of standards and procedures at the present time.

It might be stated parenthetically that it is possible that practice may be ahead of the literature in some instances. This raises possibilities for sharing experiences, in the near future, toward developing standards and procedures.

In this short paper, it is not feasible to summarize the literature. CPAs are guided by a set of ten

---

[1] *"Suggested Guidelines for the Structure and Content of Audit Guides Prepared by Federal Agencies for Use by CPAs,"* American Institute of Certified Public Accountants, 1972, 16 pp.

[2] *Ibid,* Preface, p. v.

[3] *Ibid,* p. 3.

auditing standards[4] and by Statements on Auditing Procedure issued by the American Institute's Committee on Auditing Procedure. Essentially, these are addressed to financial audits.

Academicians Have Done Little

On the academic side, it is harsh but nevertheless fair to state that very little has been done in the auditing area. Typically, an accounting curriculum has one course in auditing and it is CPA oriented. It is still considered avant-garde to cover professional ethics and statistical sampling in addition to conventional topics. Program evaluation, effectiveness, efficiency, compliance, etc. – areas which are essential to internal auditors – are almost never covered in auditing courses. The academic approach is that auditing concepts and procedures are more or less universal. The notion, therefore, is that the prospective internal auditor can study the same material as external auditors except that he will be affected differently in terms of independence.

Moreover, there has been no appreciable academic research effort, particularly in the broad areas that concern the internal auditor.

Institutional Constraints

Following the above very negative analysis, one might wonder: Where we can go from here? What can the internal auditing profession do to further interest, research and development of the broader approach?

It is important to recognize the institutional constraints on the CPA profession. That profession has been very much occupied by very demanding work in the financial auditing and reporting area. It has been on the defensive on occasion in terms of quality, competence and objectivity in the relatively better defined financial area. It is concerned about legal liability. Its reluctance to broaden scope is understandable if not admirable.

The relative lack of contributions by the academic profession is less understandable. Auditing instruction and research, however, seem to reflect the needs of CPAs. They tend to present their problems in a compelling manner. They are more aggressive in their contacts with the academic community than are internal auditors. They thereby encourage academicians to work on earnings per share, financial reporting problems of the five hundred largest companies and the like. These are important and interesting problems. Data are available. It seems to be a rather natural supply and demand response.

Internal Auditing Profession Should Take Initiative

To conclude, the development of standards and procedures for the output side of auditing is tremendously important. Help should be sought both from CPAs and academicians. Internal auditors have already taken the initiative in this field.

One very significant example of such initiative is the Federal General Accounting Office (GAO). Its recent publication on audit standards for government includes additional standards which include the

[4] These standards are included in *"Statements on Auditing Procedure No. 33,"* American Institute of CPAs. There have been more than fifty Statements on Auditing Procedure to date. No. 54 issued in November, 1972 is notable for our purpose. Its subject is *"The Auditor's Study and Evaluation of Internal Control."*

essence of the present ten standards of the CPA but go beyond them.[5] This publication resulted from cooperative efforts of many groups, including CPAs and academicians. It is a notable step forward. This work needs to be extended outside the field of government. As already suggested, internal auditors so far have taken the initiative and should continue to do so.

[5]Comptroller General of the United States, *"Standards for Audit of Governmental Organizations, Programs, Activities and Functions,"* General Accounting Office, 1972, 54 pp.

Integrating the GAO Audit Standards Into Audit Guides

Frederic A. Heim, Jr., CIA, CPA

The Internal Auditor Mar./April 1974

Through the use of audit guides, Federal agencies specify the extent of work to be performed and are better able to rely upon audits performed by public accountants or state or local audit organizations, in lieu of audits that may otherwise need to be performed by Federal auditors. The increasing importance of such guides is shown by the reference to them in the U.S. General Accounting Office (GAO) Standards for Audit of Governmental Organizations, Programs, Activities & Functions, and by the policy direction contained in recently issued Federal Management Circular 73-2.[1]

The Audit Standards provide the following:

> "An inherent assumption that underlies all the standards is that governments will cooperate in making audits in which they have mutual interests . . . Therefore, to provide the auditor with the necessary background information and to guide his judgment in the application of the accompanying standards, Federal or State agencies that request State, local, or other levels to make audits are expected to prepare broad, comprehensive audit instructions, tailored to particular programs or program areas."[2]

[1]U.S. General Services Administration, Office of Federal Management Policy, *FMC 73-2: Audit of Federal Operations and Programs by Executive Branch Agencies,* September 27, 1973.

[2]U.S. General Accounting Office, *Standards for Audit of Governmental Organizations, Programs, Activities & Functions,* June 1972, pp. 4-5.

In turn, the General Services Administration's FMC 73-2 requires that Federal agencies coordinate their audit requirements and plans with recipients of Federal aid to the maximum extent possible and that reports prepared by non-Federal auditors will be used in lieu of Federal audits if various conditions are met including the observance of the GAO Audit Standards and the audit requirements of the Federal agencies.[3]

Format of Guide

Like many Federal agencies, the Department of Commerce for many years has prepared audit guides for use by public accountants and state or local audit organizations. Although the arrangement of subject matter varies among the guides, they are usually developed in accordance with guidelines suggested by the American Institute of Certified Public Accountants (AICPA).[4]

Three of the most important elements of the guide, i.e., the audit objectives, the audit program and the report sections are discussed in the following paragraphs based on experience in the development of the initial Department of Commerce audit guide that incorporated the GAO Audit Standards.[5]

[3]FMC 73-2, *op. cit.*, p. 4.

[4]*Suggested Guidelines for the Structure and Content of Audit Guides Prepared by Federal Agencies For Use by CPAs* (New York: American Institute of Certified Public Accountants, 1972).

[5]U.S. Department of Commerce, Office of Audits, *Accounting System Survey and Audit Guide for Office of Minority Business Enterprise Contracts and Grants* February, 1973.

Audit Objectives

This section contains a concise description of the objectives to be achieved by the audits, including the identification of areas of primary interest. Prior to issuance of the GAO Audit Standards, the scope usually was limited to a financial and compliance review to determine (1) whether financial operations were properly conducted, (2) whether the financial reports of the audited entity were presented fairly and (3) whether the entity had complied with applicable laws, contracts, regulations and Federal agency instructions.

However, since the issuance of the GAO Audit Standards, Federal audit guides regularly will require a substantially broader scope of work. This broader scope will include reviews for efficiency and economy of operations and for program results. The efficiency and economy review is to determine whether the entity is managing or utilizing its resources (personnel, property, space, and so forth) in an economical and efficient manner, and to determine the causes of any inefficiencies or uneconomical practices. In addition, the audits will determine whether the desired program results or benefits are being achieved and whether the objectives established by Congress or other authorizing body are being met.

Audit Program

For the Office of Minority Business Enterprise (OMBE) guide, two programs were developed. The first was a "Survey Questionnaire" which was divided into two parts; (1) administrative controls and (2) accounting controls. The administrative controls section of the questionnaire provides, for example, for a review of the entity's organizational structure, the authorization and approval process, and its financial planning and use of operating budgets. The questionnaire is applied during the first four months of an entity's initial OMBE contract or grant period and is updated as part of the annual audit.

The other program is for use in the annual and final audit of each contract or grant. It is divided into the three main parts and their subparts as follows:

Part I – *Financial and Compliance*

Part II — *Efficiency and Economy* including: (1) adequacy of organizational structure; (2) existence of excess personnel; (3) utilization of space and equipment; and (4) purchase vs. lease of equipment.

Part III – *Program Results* including: (1) preparation of a time-phased program plan; (2) reporting of progress in achieving established goals; (3) accuracy of reports of program accomplishments and expenses; and (4) verification of services to clients including the quality thereof.

Considering the expanded audit scope and the likelihood that many of the auditors who will do the work may not have performed reviews in the area of efficiency and economy or in the evaluation of program results, substantial background data and specific audit instructions are needed to guide the auditor.

Audit Report

The format to use in reporting on the full scope audit envisioned in the GAO Audit Standards initially presented some problems. It was felt desirable to obtain a single report that would cover all the various aspects of work accomplished. Therefore, mindful of the public accountant's standards for reporting as contained in the AICPA's Statement on Auditing Procedures,[6] the format of a report was devised in modular form. It consists of a transmittal letter with a brief introduction in one paragraph, a statement of audit objectives and a short description of the audit work performed in the second, and a listing of attachments in the third.

A separate attachment is provided for each of the areas to be reported upon as follows: (1) accounting system survey, (2) financial activities, (3) compliance with contract terms and program instructions, (4) efficiency and economy of operations, and (5) program results.

By use of such attachments, the full scope of work in each area can be included in a separate section of the report along with the results of audit in that area and the results of the auditor's discussion with organization officials concerning that segment of the audit.

Coordination and Testing

The final phase of guide development consisted of its coordination with the AICPA and field testing by the office staff. In the development of the OMBE Survey and Audit Guide we also had it tested by a public accounting firm in the audit of a designated contractor.

---

[6] *Codification of Auditing Standards and Procedures 1, Statement of Auditing Standards* (New York: American Institute of Certified Public Accountants, 1973)

Conclusion

To properly integrate the GAO Audit Standards into an audit guide, the following are needed:

(1.) Thorough knowledge of program operations and management needs;

(2.) Expansion of traditional coverage of administrative controls to include, (a) review of the means used for establishment of objectives and goals, (b) organization of the entity, (c) its allocation and use of resources, (d) the measurement of progress, and (e) the controls used to assure attainment of established goals; and

(3.) Determination of the best means of accomplishing the efficiency and economy review and of evaluating whether desired program results are achieved.

Considering the wide diversity of Federal programs and needs of the various interested parties, each guide must be not only tailored to the special requirements of the program involved, but designed to provide the information needed by each interested group.

Local Auditing in Transition — GAO Standards

Lloyd F. Hara

The Internal Auditor Sept./Oct. 1973

During the past year, many events have occurred which emphasize the need for increased governmental accountability in order to maintain and restore public confidence. These incidents, many of which are unrelated but nevertheless added together, have placed all public officials on a potential powder-keg. The citizenry is seeking assurances that government will be restored to normalcy and a high level of public trust. The auditor, as the public "watchdog," has an important role, especially at local government level, to bring about a general feeling of "fair play" and to assist in preserving our democratic government (the U.S. Government) as we know it.

One can cite a few factors as to why the local auditor should pursue a broader scope of activity:

- Government activity is becoming more open with the passage of open meeting provisions and public disclosure laws. Public officials are placed in a "fish bowl." A diligent press demands information so as to keep the public better informed. An example is the recent Congressional investigation of 1972 campaign activities. In past years such information might have been withheld from the public.

- The tax revolt has caused many citizens to closely examine government tax policy and expenditures.
- The shift of power from the Federal Government to local and state government through revenue sharing brings the citizen even closer to local fiscal and program decisions. Concomitantly, the Federal Government expects greater accountability by local officials in the use of such funds. This reverses the former roles played by Federal and local officials.
- The anticipated passage of special revenue sharing and the phasing out of programs, like the community action programs and model cities, have caused local politicians and officials to become more concerned with accountability.
- There is a changing attitude within the bureaucracy to more readily accept change, as many established officials retire and are replaced by a new generation of young, bright, highly educated, eager and industrious administrators.
- The issuance of the General Accounting Office's *Standards for Audit of Governmental Organizations, Programs, Activities and Functions* probably will do much to enhance the necessity for strong auditing programs at the local level. The broad scope of audit that includes the traditional legal-fiscal compliance audit, but adds the economy and efficiency and program effectiveness elements, now promotes the auditor to financial and management expert.

Within the government auditing fraternity, the publication of the GAO audit standards should be acknowledged as a major achievement to upgrade the profession. Many people have recognized the need for such standards for a long time. Their publication has spurred a new thrust to adopt similar standards throughout the accounting and auditing profession. However, it is clearly recognized that the establishment of such standards does not mean that all auditors will comply with them. Today, compliance with the standards is voluntary. In the future, one may expect compliance to become mandatory.

Many local auditors are elected. As a result, they may not possess minimum qualifications and so find that compliance with the standards is not in their best interest. However, the key question is whether the official is aware of such standards and makes decisions with a full understanding of the consequences of such decisions. Because of being under them for too short a time, many local officials still consider the benefits to be too intangible to adopt the standards.

Aside from the political practicality of adopting the standards, there is the problem of attracting qualified and competent people into government auditing. This is critical in the smaller, out-of-the-way places, but larger governments also may have difficulty holding good people. It would be desirable, since these are national standards, for the

Federal Government to encourage and fund an intergovernmental exchange program for auditors, whereby Federal, state and local auditors could receive additional training and experience.

An outgrowth of the standards and of an exchange program would be the improvement of audit coordination. How often does one encounter parochial attitudes of not relinquishing any authority nor allowing others to perform one's work? But, when all auditors follow agreed upon standards, then a level of professional confidence between auditors can be established. Also, it may become easier to avoid duplication of audit effort.

Organization and Staff Training

Operating under an expanded audit concept, organization and skills both become very important. It is difficult to suggest a specific size staff since much is dependent on the size of the organization and the support given to the auditor by top management. In smaller jurisdictions, some audit functions can be performed by existing staff, such as administrative assistants to mayors or county supervisors or even by the staff of the finance director or comptroller.

For those considering a comprehensive audit program, an audit staff of not less than three professionals is required to adequately cover the range of activity typical of local government. They should work as a team. This team effort improves the quality of analysis, maintains job continuity, allows for timely reports and provides a mechanism to integrate various skills. The team is tailored to meet the requirements of a job through selection of members who may possess skills such as industrial engineering, psychology, economics and accounting. Because of this cross-mixing of skills, the team views problems from varying professional vantage points aside from the traditional fiscal position. Team members are also cognizant of the social and operational aspects of running a government.

A continuing educational program is considered vital and may consist of both in-house and outside training. Examples of in-house training include report writing, use of data processing-audit software programs and specific analytical techniques. Each office should tailor its training program to enhance the skills already possessed by the staff and to accommodate the type of work that is expected to be performed. Since auditing is now becoming an avant-garde activity, it demands a continuing education program.

The GAO audit standards take on added importance when it is seen that these standards can be expected to affect the local auditor in matters of organization, qualifications and training.

As he improves in these fields, the local auditor can expect to play an important role in:

- Achieving greater accountability.
- Identifying cost savings to control taxes.
- Preventing potential corruption and fraud.
- Assisting in better decision making.
- Improving government credibility.

These activities are of utmost importance to every member of the community. And, because of this, it behooves each local auditor to awaken to his true potential, prepare himself for it and take his rightful place in the scheme of things.

Editor's note — A paragraph on independence from Hara's letter accompanying his article was so appropriate to his subject that it is printed here.

"The GAO audit standards emphasize a broadened scope of auditing. In so doing, some problems are raised regarding true independence. Can an auditor be truly independent and yet involve himself in management and, occasionally, policy questions? It becomes very difficult to disengage himself and objectively examine whether or not his recommendations are followed. Perhaps this may become a matter of greater concern as the overall aspect of management improves and others perform analysis and management evaluation. No doubt, GAO's involvement with the Congress —especially its growing involvement in advising Congress on specific legislation and performing staff work—makes the comptroller general uneasy, as it does me in working with our local county council. However, I feel that the GAO audit standards are so vital that they should be applied as vigorously as possible, even though doing so brings one face to face with severe problems in maintaining true independence."

Lloyd F. Hara,
King County Auditor

Can the Government Internal Auditor Be Independent?

Daniel Paul, CPA

The Internal Auditor July/Aug. 1973

At the outset, it is important to distinguish between an internal auditor in private industry and the Governmental Internal Auditor.

Private internal auditors, consider internal auditing as an independent appraisal activity within an organization for the review of accounting, financial and other operations as a basis for service to management. They look upon their operation as a form of managerial control, which functions by measuring and evaluating the effectiveness of other controls. They believe and rightly so, that the head of the internal auditing department should be responsible to an officer of sufficient rank in the organization as will assure a broad scope of activities and adequate consideration of and effective action on the findings or recommendations made by him.[1]

Responsibilities of Government Internal Auditors

While the Government internal auditor may have responsibilities similar to those of the private internal auditor, he must also examine accounts with ending balances and perform balance sheet audits. In instances where the smaller governmental units do not have separate internal audit divisions or departments, most states require a certified public accountant to perform the balance sheet type audit. The internal auditing that is done in these smaller units is generally that part of internal accounting control utilizing internal check procedures.

This presentation is concerned with the auditor responsible to the public and its elected representatives to see that financial interests of the public are protected.

The National Committee on Governmental Accounting in its 1968 publication defines Auditing of Governmental Units as follows:

> *"Auditing is the process of examining documents, records, reports, systems of internal control, accounting and financial procedures, and other evidence for one or more of the following purposes:*
>
> *"(1) To ascertain whether the statements prepared from the accounts present fairly the financial position and results of financial operations of the constituent funds and balanced account groups of the governmental unit in accordance with generally accepted accounting principles applicable to governmental units and on a basis consistent with that of the preceding years;*
>
> *"(2) To determine the propriety, legality, and mathematical accuracy of a governmental unit's financial transactions;*
>
> *"(3) To ascertain whether all financial transactions have been properly recorded; and*
>
> *"(4) To ascertain the stewardship of public officials who handle and are responsible for financial resources of a governmental unit."*

Who Perform Government Audits?

There are generally three groups of auditors who perform governmental audits: (1) the auditor, who is on the staff of the governmental unit, (2) the State audit agency and (3) the private CPA. Independence of the auditor is essential whether he is elected, appointed or hired under contract. When a governmental unit has both an internal audit department and an obligation to hire an outside independent auditor; the scope of the outside auditors and the resultant cost of the contract will depend, among other things, on the degree of independence of the internal audit function.

State Auditor

In 1968, the state of Maryland established the position of Legislative

[1]The Institute of Internal Auditors, *"Statement of Responsibilities of the Internal Auditor."*

Auditor, required him to be a certified public accountant and required him to make a full and detailed report in writing, to a joint legislative committee on budget and audit at the conclusion of each audit he performs. Copies of audits of all subdivisions within the State are required to be forwarded to the Legislative Auditor which he may accept or reject. If unacceptable or if none has been submitted, he may conduct an audit on his own at the expense of the subdivision. This "State" auditor, therefore, has the same independence as a private auditor under contract.

City Auditor

The City of Baltimore, by charter, requires the City Auditor to be a certified public accountant and to submit all audit reports to the five members of the Board of Estimates simultaneously. Included in this group are the Mayor, President of the City Council and the Comptroller – all of whom are elected officials. In addition, the City Auditor must prepare annually a comprehensive public report of the financial position of the City; such report may be in the form of an opinion on the annual financial statement prepared by the Director of Finance.

It is obvious that the City Auditor must and does have complete independence. By agreement, the Secretary of the Board of Estimates releases the reports of the City Auditor to the public press forty-eight hours after they have been delivered to the members of the Board.

The Trend

The trend in governmental auditing agencies is in the direction of hiring professionals on the audit staffs. This is necessary for those units which by law must establish an internal independent auditing department. The generally accepted auditing standards applicable to training, audit proficiency, mental attitude, due professional care, field work and reporting; dictate the necessity of heading up and staffing the audit department with competent professional supervisors. They must be free to conduct their assignments and perform their functions as though they were auditing for private industry.

Benefits of Independence

The independent government internal auditor can be the most economical protection device the public taxpayer has. Through proper legislative enactment, he should: have authority to hire a proficient professional staff, report to a representative group or body other than those collectively managing the agency or department audited, have access to all records and documents necessary to conduct his examination, have authority to utilize data processing facilities as an audit tool, where available.

The independent government internal auditor can readily observe inventory takings; keep on top of new laws as they affect financial accounting responsibilities; attend governing board or legislative meetings; be available as consultant to government on legislative or policy matters.

Conclusion

All that has been previously said pertaining to staffing an independent internal auditor agency on a professional basis would be superfluous if governmental auditing salaries were not competitive with the private sector.

The aforementioned comments lead to the conclusion that the governmental internal auditor can be independent – and should be.

A Case of Independence in Auditing

Harvey M. Rose, CPA

The Internal Auditor December 1976

It is my strong belief that if government auditors report the facts properly and make appropriate recommendations, their audits will produce hard cash savings for taxpayers. By savings, I mean a reduction in expenditures, an increase in revenues, or an increase in the value of additional public services without an increase in staff costs.

Under all circumstances, auditors attempt to report the facts. In the case of the San Francisco Board of Supervisors, for example, the budget director and analyst is permitted to gather and report the facts regardless of what those facts might disclose.

In a sense, auditors, as government agents, are the instruments of measuring cost efficiencies. Highly trained accountants have perfected skills that are not only useful but also vital to all of us. Their skills will keep the human race from being buried by burgeoning bureaucracies and strangled by reels of red tape.

But those skills are useless unless they operate in an atmosphere of independence unchecked by political interests. It is imperative that we demand independence since public officials must base their decisions on intellectual truth and factual honesty.

In order for us to get the facts, do a job, obtain job satisfaction, make feasible recommendations, and effect economies, the elected policy makers must permit us to operate in an open atmosphere. With the auditor general of California, this was not always the case. An open and independent atmosphere, free of politics, motivates auditors to do the best job possible for the taxpayers they represent.

As auditor general in 1974, I was frequently accused by some Republicans of being under the control of the Democratic legislature. In 1975, I was accused by some Democrats of issuing reports

This is a highly controversial case. Rose's article vividly illustrates potential problems with independence, an area from which it is difficult to obtain case studies. The Institute of Internal Auditors takes no position on this case.

on behalf of Republicans. I was accused of being naive in my relations with the California legislature. If attempting to disregard politics in reporting the facts is being naive, then I plead guilty.

The auditor general submits reports to the Joint Legislative Audit Committee. The Committee sets the policy. What it does with audit recommendations is the Committee's prerogative. But the decision on how to conduct the audit and what the final audit report will contain must remain with the auditor.

I have emphasized to my staff that my objective is to make a profit. We should come up with recommendations from at least a majority of our audits which, if properly implemented, will result in savings that exceed the costs of the audit. However, we must be objective and not load reports or manufacture findings or deficiencies. If there is no room for improvement and if the agency is doing a great job, the report will reflect that.

I did not want the auditor general's office to be seen as just another bureaucracy. I wanted it to be recognized for the savings the office recouped.

No savings accrued to the taxpayers, however, by sending out a press release which appeared below a headline in the *San Diego Evening Tribune* saying, "San Diego Gas and Electric Rate Hikes Face State Probe."

Prior to this press release, we had obtained complete cooperation from San Diego Gas and Electric. When the headline hit, San Diego Gas and Electric almost kicked us out, literally. The auditor general's staff has not been back since that time. When the company sued to block the audit, the chairman of the Joint Legislative Audit Committee was more concerned about ordering the auditor general's staff to justify a change in venue to his hometown of San Diego than about having the audit proceed. This is not independence.

It has been the legacy of government to cultivate multifaceted bureaucracies in trying to respond to human needs. It is our job to make sure that those bureaucracies are useful and efficient. It is also our duty to recommend that they be altered or eliminated if they are not.

Unlike CPA's, whose clients seek assistance, government auditors are adversaries of the audited agency and other interested parties.

The California state management audit reports have not won many friends. Making friends, however, was not one of my audit responsibilities. I was responsible for reporting the facts even at the expense of making enemies.

As auditor general and a member of the American Institute of Certified Public Accountants, I fully subscribed to the Institute's generally accepted auditing standard which states:

> *In all matters relating to the assignment, an independence in mental attitude is to be maintained by the auditor or auditors.*

This independence is vital if our audit reports are to benefit taxpayers. As I define it, independence does not mean disregarding the policies and procedures of the Joint Legislative Audit Committee. It does mean being able to conduct audits free of political interference.

While I was the state auditor general, the chairman of the Joint Legislative Audit Committee stated that I was a political appointee and that I should conduct my affairs accordingly. For the record, I applied for the position of California auditor general through an ad in the *Wall Street Journal.* I was one of 210 applicants. This list was narrowed to five by the state legislative analyst and legislative counsel.

I never viewed myself as a political appointee. For me to have conducted my affairs in that fashion would have rendered me useless to the people I was hired to serve: the members of the Joint Legislative Audit Committee and the taxpayers of California.

After I accused the chairman of interfering with the auditor general's office, he stated that I was being fired for giving myself several unauthorized pay increases in violation of my contract. Subsequently, he made what he called a "detailed investigation" and issued a report concluding that his accusations were confirmed. He reported that I would be billed $637 for the unauthorized salary increases. Incidentally, these cost of living increases had been approved more than one year prior to the chairman's accusations.

I filed a claim against the state of California which has now been *settled. The settlement stated,*

> *It is understood and agreed that Mr. Rose did not at any time during his employment as auditor general allocate to himself or others, or receive, any unauthorized wages or salary increases or other employment benefits.*

Not only was I not billed for $637, but, pursuant to the settlement agreement, the legislature paid me $12,000 for the amount due me under my contract. The $12,000 included payment for the so-called unauthorized salary increases which had been withheld. The chairman termed the settlement a *nuisance settlement.*

I believe that taxpayers are entitled to independent audits, free of political interference, and I intend to produce such audits.

4
operational audit concepts

Operational auditing in government is full-scope auditing that includes the examination and evaluation of:

- Financial aspects
- Compliance with policy, plans, procedures, laws, and regulations
- The efficiency and economy with which governmental resources are used
- The effectiveness with which program results are achieved

This broad-scope audit is described in the first of the GAO audit standards. It is the characteristic that sets most internal auditing apart from the traditional audit performed by the CPA or independent public accountant — predominantly pointed toward the certification of financial statements, the examination of financial controls, and the safeguarding of assets.

Thus, the operational concepts are more management oriented and serve to evaluate management activities as well as review the financial operations. The full-scope audit normally includes all four elements described above, although audits may contain any one or more of the elements. One factor determining the scope of the audit is that there must be a positive relationship between cost of the audit and the potential benefits to be derived.

Expanding the scope of internal auditing is not done without problems. First, the audit staff must possess a new array of skills to provide expertise in management and in substantive areas beyond financial aspects. Second, the credibility of the audit staff in these new areas may not be readily acknowledged. This could cause lack of support by top management and resistance from the auditee. It must be clearly understood that the auditor is reviewing management controls rather than the substance to which these controls are applied.

Management itself has a dominant part to play in internal auditing. It participates in these ways:

- Determines basic audit policy
- Sets the scope of the audit
- Provides the auditor with access to records and people
- Orients the total organization as to the functions and potential benefits of internal audit
- Provides the auditor with necessary resources
- Directs action based on audit findings
- Establishes follow-up procedures to determine if directives were followed (usually an audit activity)

However, remember that within the framework described above the auditor has the sole responsibility to:

- Establish procedures for audit work
- Plan the audit operation
- Direct and supervise the audit staff
- Expand the scope of individual audits where circumstances dictate
- Determine items material enough to report
- Determine frequency, method, and structure of reports
- Coordinate audit efforts with the auditee and other audit organizations
- Maintain a quality control operation over the audit process

The audit process itself is carried out through the use of a sequence of well-established audit activities. These activities include:

1. Developing audit guidelines to establish parameters within which audits should be conducted. (Audit procedures are an integral part of this activity.)
2. Planning for the employment of audit resources. (The audit schedule, identifying audits to be made, manpower needs, and time, is a basic part of this activity.)
3. Using the preliminary audit survey. (This survey includes the study of background material, interviews with management and workers, on-site or walk-through inspections, and reporting.)
4. Conducting the examination and evaluation phase. (This activity is the in-depth study of areas disclosed by the survey as being potential sources of audit findings.)
5. Continuing supervision, review, and control of audit work to assure consistent quality of audits.
6. Reporting the results of the audit activity.
7. Maintaining an evaluation of the overall audit process.

The following articles describe these operational concepts and activities in the abstract and then discuss their application to specific segments of governmental audit activity. A discussion of the audit of operational controls and nonfinancial data by Richard J. Griffin, assistant comptroller for auditing, U.S. Energy Research and Development Agency, sets the stage for the chapter by identifying the basic steps of control auditing. Dr. Richard E. Brown, legislative post auditor of Kansas, carries the audit concept further by explaining its application to program evaluation.

Two articles discuss audit activity as it is applied to two progressive audit operations in the federal government. Gerald J. Greenway, National Aeronautics and Space Administration, writes about operational auditing including objectives, its multidisciplined approach, and the development of good working relationships in that agency. John W. Fawsett, U.S. Army Audit Agency, describes a performance analysis and planning (PAP) innovation that provides for continuous monitoring of operational activities by the agency.

Two articles describe operational auditing in state government. Dr. Lennis Knighton, formerly professor of accounting and public administration at Brigham Young University, and now auditor-general of Utah, reports the results of a study of operational auditing in states and points out activities that can help improve this auditing. Former legislative auditor of Georgia, Ernest B. Davis, describes the staffing and operation of the Georgia auditor's office and specifically tells about a specialized staff for conducting nonfinancial audits.

The importance and the position of internal auditing in local governments is described by Dr. Meyer Drucker, formerly of the University of North Carolina at Charlotte, and now at the University of South Carolina. Lloyd F. Hara of King County, Seattle, Washington, discusses scope, independence, and strategy as it applies to local audits. Thomas J. Falstad tells how a new operational audit organization was started in Hennepin County, Minneapolis, Minnesota.

An educational aspect of performance auditing is described by James M. Williams, formerly of the University of Tennessee, and now an assistant director of the Municipal Finance Officers Association. The chapter concludes with a provocative piece by Dr. William Campfield, "Is Auditing a *Sine Qua Non* in the Management Process?" This article questions the intrinsic value of operational auditing and provides a very interesting answer.

Audit of Operational Controls and Nonfinancial Data

Richard J. Griffin, Jr., CPA

The Internal Auditor June 1976

Any operation, whether it be administrative or technical, requires controls to function effectively. The absence, inappropriateness, inadequacy of such controls, or the failure of personnel to follow prescribed controls will likely result in an inefficient and unnecessarily costly operation or one that fails to fully achieve management's objectives.

It is the auditor's responsibility to ascertain whether any of the foregoing conditions exist, the adverse impact on the activity under review, and the corrective action needed.

In approaching an audit of operational controls, all activities of an organization can be divided into one of two broad categories: (1) those directly related to fulfilling program objectives and (2) those that are supportive in nature. An example of the former would be providing adequate safeguards for the handling and disposal of radioactive waste. An example of the latter would be the various administrative functions such as contracting and procurement, personnel and payroll, management of capital assets, and the like.

Basic Steps

In conducting any audit of operational controls, there are certain basic steps that must be taken whether the activity being examined relates to direct fulfillment of a program objective or to one of the support services. These steps include:

1. Obtaining a working knowledge of the activity through reading pertinent material and holding discussions with key personnel
2. Understanding the organizational structure for carrying out the activity
3. Developing flowcharts showing how the various responsibilities are discharged
4. Identifying key control points in the activity

This basic background information is necessary for the auditor to intelligently select those features of an operation on which he should concentrate his efforts as well as to help place any audit findings in proper perspective.

While the particular audit steps will vary depending upon the personnel, organization, and objectives of the activity under review, we present below some of the key features of auditing program controls and controls of support services:

Operating Program

There are four principal matters to consider in assessing the adequacy of program controls:

Whether specific goals and objectives have been established for each program and subprogram. If the purpose of a program is not identified in specific terms, no sound basis exists for measuring progress toward achieving this purpose. For example, it would not be possible to determine the accomplishment of a goal that was stated in such general terms as "to conduct as much research, to educate as many individuals, or to build as many facilities as possible with the funds provided."

That related criteria have been developed to permit measurement of results and accomplishments against the preestablished goals. It is important that the means of ascertaining that goals have been achieved also be clearly defined in order that the method for measurement be understood and utilized by those responsible for doing so.

That the existing management review system provides for comparison of results against the established measurement criteria. While the auditor would make such comparisons as a part of the audit, an essential operating control toward assuring that goals are being achieved is a provision for internal "policing" of the operation by those with the adequate technical knowledge to do so.

That comparisons prescribed by the established measurement system were, in fact, made and appropriate and timely action was taken where indicated to be necessary.

Support Services

Normally, written policies and procedures will have been developed covering each of the service activities. These may represent standards developed externally: the Federal Procurement regulations as well as internally generated requirements. The auditor's starting point is to ascertain that this body of controls is being complied with. However, two additional steps are essential.

First, in cases where procedures are not being observed, the auditor should ascertain why this situation came about and what adverse effects, if any, resulted from the noncompliance. It may well be that the established procedure has outlived its usefulness or that it is not applicable in the situation under review. It also may be that noncompliance did not result in any adverse effects which also raises a question as to the need for the requirement.

The second consideration is the impact and relationship of support service deficiencies disclosed by the audit to the fulfillment of the basic program objectives discussed above. The auditor should always ask himself, "What effect do these findings, such as delays in procurement or shortages in staff, have on achieving the basic program goals?"

In summary, the audit considerations and approaches in reviewing support service activities are somewhat different from those for operating programs. In the final analysis, however, whatever the nature of the review, the auditor should always have in mind the primary reason for an organization's existence and the effect of any lack of controls on the ability of that organization to successfully carry out its mission.

Program Evaluation Audits

Dr. Richard E. Brown

The Internal Auditor October 1976

In the face of the growing need of legislators and the public for better information and demands for increased efficiency in the public sector, there is an ever-increasing and very practical challenge for auditors.

The extent to which governmental program evaluation can be integrated into a modern auditing operation and serve to meet the new demands for this evaluation work remains to be proved. The techniques and substance of program evaluation require diverse analytical perspectives and wide-ranging skills that have not traditionally joined ranks in audit staffs.

The use of single-purpose legislative program evaluation staffs in a number of states like Illinois, Virginia, and New York, which are generally divorced from the audit organization, illustrates the timeliness and relevancy of the issue. State auditors are being asked frequently by legislators:Can you do more of this program evaluation or performance work? Are you able to take on this program audit activity?

Recent and current changes in governmental auditing must be reflected in the qualifications and backgrounds of practitioners at the federal, state, and local levels. The modern auditing operation increasingly includes financial and compliance auditing as well as operations and program-effectiveness auditing. Internally, audit staffs are often segregated along these lines — Illinois, Kansas, and Minnesota illustrate this approach. For many reasons — performing an occasional truly comprehensive audit, minimizing potential duplication of audit work, etc. — cooperation between these staffs is essential. Indeed, the second general standard for governmental auditing presented in GAO's *Standards for Audit of Governmental Organizations, Programs, Activities and Functions* is:

> *The auditors assigned to perform the audit must collectively possess adequate professional proficiency for the tasks required (p.13, author's italics).*

Later this "yellow book" discusses a wide variety of skills and states: "The qualifications mentioned herein should apply to the skills of the audit organizations as a whole and not necessarily to individual auditors."

These statements raise the now well-recognized issue of the need for varied audit skills, and reference is made to the possible need for cooperative audits by different audit organizations. Unfortunately, not much is said about how to organize the various skills on an audit job.

Recent Developments and Changing Perspectives

The trend toward broader audit organizational capabilities involves the cooperation of professionals with diverse training and often with differing points of view (even toward the general approach to auditing). Common among government audit organizations today is a staff trained not only in accounting, business administration, finance, operations research but also in economics and other social sciences, public administration, and statistical analysis. For example, the growing interest in surveys and questionnaires aimed at obtaining comments from large numbers of people, has brought with it a new understanding of the need for a fairly sophisticated grasp of statistical sampling and survey techniques. This, in turn, includes knowledge about the very specialized area of questionnaire design and, for example, how one asks questions to elicit fairly objective responses without "loading the deck."

There has been justifiable criticism of auditors for some significant shortcomings in these and other such specialized areas. To take the illustration a step further, program evaluation auditing will sometimes be unable to avoid the use of sophisticated statistical techniques and the aid of a computer in following through with the analytical work related to these techniques.

Blending these skills in the production of meaningful audit work is no mean accomplishment. Moreover, the literature is not paying enough attention to the problem.

To arrive at an answer to the question of organizing audit work in this new setting, one must examine some differences between the terms "program auditing" (or "program results") and "program evaluation." One knowledgeable practitioner argues that the differences are real:

> *"Perhaps it should be said that program evaluation and program auditing are basically similar in their objectives, differing primarily in their origins and their techniques. Generally speaking, program auditing has evolved from the profession of accountancy and from finance and compliance auditing, while program evaluation is derived primarily from the social sciences.*
>
> *Another difference is that program evaluators generally will go further than auditors (1) to construct program objectives where statutory and documentary sources are vague and (2) to question existing program objectives if their research raises doubts about them.*
>
> *Another possible differentation is that auditing is generally oriented toward negative findings — toward pursuing the problems and irregularities in the system — whereas evaluation seeks a more comprehensive view of a program or system (while at the same time , hopefully, identifying the problems in it). Another possibility is that program evaluation devotes more effort to research design than auditing has tended to and seeks to identify impact and results in terms of social and economic variables or indicators with which auditors are often uncomfortable.*
>
> *Finally, auditing and evaluation generally employ different techniques with evaluation relying on comparisons between groups, on quasi-experiments, on attitudinal surveys, and on statistical techniques rarely attempted by auditors."**

This appears to be a reasonable list of some of the differences between program auditing and program evaluation. Close inspection, however, suggests that such differences may be quickly reduced or even eliminated as adjustments are made. For example, there is growing recognition that social scientists can play an important role in auditing. Furthermore, the techniques ascribed to evaluators — statistical techniques, attitudinal surveys, and group comparisons — can, with care, be built into the work of any good audit group.

Significantly, Chadwin notes:

> *The problem with some of these comments is that there are, of course, some auditors (notably LCER in New York and the legislative auditor in Hawaii) who already use most or all of these techniques ... Furthermore, I suspect that, over time, the differentiations may tend to blur even further.*

A Proposed Solution

My experience leads me to conclude that, indeed, the "blurring" referred to above will continue. Perhaps, this is why I feel the phrase "program evaluation audits" has a very sensible ring to it (in any event, it is a compromise term; and state auditors, among other things, quickly learn how to compromise).

On the other hand, I would be sorry if anyone reads my remarks to suggest that a traditional audit agency, unchanged, could really perform program evaluation audits. I do not believe they can.

Even a casual sampling of that work points up the need for different skills, different approaches, and, to some extent, different people.† Moreover, I would argue that it is

* Comments contained in a letter in November of 1974 from Mark L. Chadwin, director, Illinois Fiscal and Economic Review Commission.

† For a discussion of this topic, see Richard E. Brown and Ray D. Pethtel, "A Matter of Facts: State Legislative Performance Audit-

very difficult, perhaps impossible, to do justice to such important work while fulfilling the statutory responsibilities of many audit agencies by neatly merging all such audit work into ongoing audit terms.

Unfortunately, it is not that easy. I suspect, like so many easy solutions, one would end up dissatisfied with all audit products, regardless of name. In addition, an agency would probably damage its financial audit cycle.

We in the Kansas Legislative Division of Post Audit are attempting to avoid some of these pitfalls. Other problems will arise, but I believe they will not be as serious.

A financial-compliance audit branch headed by a CPA and a program evaluation audit branch headed by a PhD economist, thus far comprise our main thrust for becoming a comprehensive audit function. The financial audit branch consists of about 20 accounting and finance specialists; the program branch has ten auditors with degrees in public and business administration and the social sciences. My experience suggests that a full-scope audit encompassing all three audit elements will be a rare thing, indeed. Such comprehensive audits are by definition so complex that they overwhelm rather than inform and aid decision makers. The capability for such work exists, however; and on occasion, a full-scope report will be issued. The middle area, operations audit work, is to be covered by careful coordination between the two branches. It will show up in the reports of both branches. Interchange of personnel between branches is a key part of the system.

The attempt to broaden financial and compliance auditing into operations auditing on a regular is also underway. As long as financial-compliance audit work is not downgraded, having those involved in these engagements constructively cover operational issues is invaluable.

This effort, however, is constrained by practical considerations. The rush of the statutory biennial financial audit cycle, applied to nearly 130 state agencies in the case of Kansas, precludes extensive operations investigations given present staff resources.

The literature and theory about operations auditing do not address this basic problem. This is a major reason why it is probably not possible to have a staff covered under a statutory charge to do financial auditing and program audit work. Program audit work is time-consuming and absorbs considerable staff resources. By its very nature, it would probably cause a decline in financial audit coverage. It appears that most legislators are not interested in such a development.

What the Trends Indicate

Indeed, a dangerous situation may be developing: the trend to increase program audit activity at the expense of financial-compliance expense of financial-compliance work seems to be taking hold nationwide. Might this trend not lead to grave consequences for the profession?

For example, to move financial auditing to a no-year audit cycle too quickly or to merge it with the more

---

ing," *Public Administration Review* July/August 1974. Some evaluation case studies are presented in Mark L. Chadwin (ed.), *Legislative Program Evaluation In the States: Four Cases,* Eagleton Institute of Politics, Rutgers University, August 1974. This material discusses the significant differences between evaluation work and traditional audit work and much current operational audit work.

exciting and newer kinds of audit work too fully are trends which all of us, regardless of discipline, should view very carefully.

The contribution of program evaluation auditing, both potential and real, cannot be dismissed. But the same can be said of traditional financial-compliance audit work. Both are essential.

Integrating the two staffs in the audit agency, given the present constraints in most states, is likely to produce a hybrid which is unsatisfactory from all points of view.

The continued development of comprehensive audit capabilities should be encouraged within the well-coordinated environment of the audit agency but separate internal staffing arrangements should be made.

This article is adapted from a paper presented at the 34th International Conference of The Institute of Internal Auditors in Dallas, Texas, June 17, 1975. The author wishes to acknowledge the assistance of John Kiefhaber of the Kansas Legislative Division of Post Audit for his assistance in revising the paper.

Operating Auditing at NASA

Gerald J. Greenway

The Internal Auditor Mar./April 1973

The NASA Management Audit Office operates on a decentralized basis with field offices located at the agency's major field centers. These centers are guided by headquarters policy but each enjoys considerable freedom within the limits of policy directives. Although the field audit offices are organizationally an arm of headquarters, in final practice they really complement the center organizations. Each field office develops its annual audit program to respond to the needs of the center at which located and encourages the involvement of center management in the planning process. The audit offices perform the barest minimum of compliance type reviews, concentrating instead on the efficiency and economy of internal center operations.

Audit Objectives

The major function of NASA auditors is to ascertain that the financial and administrative systems are sound and operating as intended. We must be familiar with the organizational controls, statements of objectives, general policy statements and directives, procedures for operations, standards of performance and other control media over the entire area of business operations.

In performing operational audits we have relied as much as possible upon modern audit tools. Computers are available, of course, and statistical sampling lends itself to many audits. Most helpful also is a library of studies and analyses on subjects related to the operations of NASA.

Auditors cannot become experts in every field or function to be audited. However, within NASA, every operational area has people trained and experienced in the most advanced technologies. As one aid in analyzing and evaluating technical operations we have developed a multi-disciplined audit technique. This technique uses a team composed of auditors, plus operational specialists from engineering, technological, and administrative fields. We use a mix of professions sufficient to provide specialized evaluation in all areas under review. The specialists are used on a consultant basis rather than team members.

The multi-disciplined approach has been used extensively within NASA to conduct management investigations and scientific inquiries into various technical areas. This approach has usually employed a panel of representatives from various NASA centers, each with specific knowledge and experience in the subject area. Thus, the multi-disciplined approach seemed to be a logical way to increase the scope and depth of an audit without staffing engineers as full-time members of the audit organization.

In addition to greater penetration in a technological area, there is less resistance to recommended changes when supported by operational experts, and faster response to recommended changes. Identification and commendation for accomplished changes are always reported.

Effective use of the multi-discipline audit technique requires the full support of management officials. Accordingly, sufficient introductory explanations must be given to these individuals as well as the management officials directly involved with audited areas. Management officials have generally agreed that the auditors should retain their objectivity by using the assigned specialists in a consultant capacity rather than as full-team members; and that the auditors should retain their independence in controlling the audit and writing the audit report. In addition to full support from management officials, proper selection of specialists to participate with the auditors is of vital importance.

In auditing the conversion of Apollo launch facilities to accommodate Skylab launch vehicles we have applied the multi-discipline audit technique. Basically, participation by the non-auditor team members has been to explain the work in his area, to select other personnel to be interviewed, to interpret information developed during interviews, to relate the segment under review to the total operation, and to aid the auditors in understanding and evaluating the system.

A person with an engineering background is preferable in evaluating the necessity for an engineering action. He can interpret engineering requirements, evaluate the need for or feasibility of alternate methods of satisfying requested changes, provide technical evaluation of material and personnel requirements, and evaluate the extent of quality inspection requirements.

A report based upon a multi-discipline team effort must have a positive, helpful tone, and avoid being negative and critical. With strong and active support from management, credit should be given for changes accomplished during the course of the audit.

Working Relationships

Good working relationships are the result of past cooperation and mutual support between center officials and auditors. Center management officials accept operational audit reports as an objective source of management information and visibility, and consider the audit staff as a part of the total NASA team. The multi-discipline audit technique is one example of this mutual support and cooperation.

A good working relationship allows auditors to cross organizational lines to identify and evaluate a problem from an overall viewpoint, identify the basic cause or causes of the problem, and arrive at conclusions upon which we can base recommendations for corrective actions. This cooperative working relationship and flexibility was a contributing factor in influencing the director of audits to orient certain audits to compensate for reduced review capabilities within NASA headquarters functional management areas.

Conclusion

Decentralization of operational authority to NASA Field Centers which are, in effect, separate entities within NASA, makes it expedient for the responsibility and authority for performance of internal audits to be similarly decentralized. The audit organization uses modern tools including scientific specialists as consultants to provide comprehensive reviews and to offer constructive recommendations.

As one aid in analyzing and evaluating operations, we have developed what we call a multi-discipline audit. The multi-discipline audit team is comprised of auditors as well as specialists from engineering, technological, and administrative fields. These specialists function as consultants, rather than as full team members, partly to permit the auditors to retain an independence and objectivity toward the review. As each area is selected by the auditors, the consultant is called upon to explain the workings of his area, to select other personnel to be interviewed, to help interpret information developed during interviews, to relate the segment under review to the total operation, and to aid the auditors in understanding and evaluating the system.

Army Audit Protects with 'PAP' — You Can Too!

John W. Fawsett, CIA

The Internal Auditor May/June 1973

Improved performance in major mission areas is generally the basic objective of management audits. Toward this end, audit effort is concentrated in the mission areas, the effectiveness of operations in each area are evaluated, causes of substandard performance are determined, and realistic recommendations for improving operations are made. However, as the management auditors strive to provide better audit service in more complex operational areas, elaborate audit planning and control systems have been developed in virtually all major audit organizations. Auditable entities or functions are identified, priorities are agreed upon, the annual audit program is developed, and the entire audit staff is soon productively employed in the audit of the entities or functions that have been scheduled.

The Problem Created

Too often the auditor — and frequently the entire audit staff — is totally involved in either performing audits that were programmed several months in advance, or in performing audits specifically requested by management. This can lead to a general ignorance of current problems in urgent need of audit attention. It is essential that the auditor avoid this trap if management is to be provided with good protective audit service.

Army Audit's Solution

The U.S. Army Audit Agency has programmed audit time for continuous Performance Analysis and Planning (PAP) at several major Army activities. Key performance indicators are monitored and important projects are reviewed at each critical milestone in their development. Any significant problems disclosed are immediately reviewed in depth and recommendations are made quickly to bring the problem under control before a significant waste of dollars, manpower, or time has occurred. The results of this effort have been excellent. Many millions of dollars have been saved through identifying unneeded or defective major items before they have been standardized and procured in quantity. Although the details of the "PAP" approach were developed to fit the uniqueness of the Army's mission and organization, the general principles of the approach have universal application.

Basic Concepts of "PAP"

It is absolutely essential that a portion of the available audit time be devoted to Performance Analysis and Planning *regardless of the extent of the backlog of other audit work.* Through "PAP" efforts, problem areas should be centrally identified and controlled. The urgency of need for corrective action and the significance of the problem itself should dictate whether to proceed on an expedited "flash reporting" type basis or to defer the problem for a more comprehensive and programmed audit approach.

At least 5 to 10% of the audit organizations' available time should be devoted to Performance Analysis and Planning. At locations serviced by an audit staff of 10 to 20 auditors, at least two auditors should be assigned responsibility to "PAP." Each should be knowledgeable of the audited activity's operations and be capable of assuming auditor-in-charge responsibility for audit of identified urgent problem areas at any time. It is essential that only the better auditors be used in the "PAP" program and that the auditor who identifies the problem area lead the audit of the area to its conclusion. Where the entire audit staff consists of only one or two auditors, at least one day each two weeks should be devoted to performing "PAP." This will permit continued surveillance of operations as well as allow for immediate audit development of urgent problems.

A centralized control should be established to function as a focus point for audit leads developed as a result of the "PAP" program as well as other audit efforts. Each audit lead should be summarized on an audit lead sheet. Particular emphasis should be given to highlighting the significance and urgency of the matter being discussed. The audit lead sheets provide the supervisor with a basis for deciding whether the problem should be immediately reviewed in depth, scheduled for review at a later time, or dropped.

A major means of monitoring an activity's operations should begin with an analysis of the budget and include review of statistical, status, and other analyses type reporting already being accumulated by the activity. Recurring and special reports should be identified for continuous review. Of particular importance are the narrative analyses prepared on many reports. Significant milestones should be identified for major projects and the auditor should review the status of the projects as each milestone is reached.

In addition to analysis of reports prepared by the activities, other audit efforts should contribute input to the "PAP" program. Audit personnel not engaged directly in "PAP" should be alert for problem areas beyond their immediate area of interest for referral to auditors working on "PAP." This would include reviews at other locations or levels. Audit lead sheets should be used to furnish details on noted conditions.

All areas of major operations should be subjected to "PAP" giving particular attention to the review of items or new programs emerging or about to emerge from the planning stage and to proposed and recently accomplished procurement actions. Emphasis should be given to reviewing whether what is either planned or recently initiated meets all the major aspects of a valid requirement and is needed in the form or quantity specified. While "PAP" is productive in all stages of the procurement process, it is especially effective when directed toward management actions before the procurement is awarded. It is in this "preaward" area that the greatest opportunity exists for savings to be realized as a result of good protective audit service.

Even the best "PAP" program will not identify all the problems needing resolution – but it will ferret out the more significant or sensitive ones. Each audit organization should have an approach that produces similar results. "PAP" is the approach used by the US Army Audit Agency. And it works.

Improving Internal Auditing In State Agencies

Dr. Lennis M. Knighton

The Internal Auditor Nov./Dec. 1972

Under the sponsorship of the Washington Chapter of The Institute of Internal Auditors, a study was made recently of internal auditing in state government. As the director of that project, I was impressed with the tremendous opportunity that exists today for members of The Institute to give more vigorous and extensive leadership to the development of programs in this area. The purpose of this paper is to propose and briefly discuss a few ways in which this leadership might be organized to be most effective.

Current Status of Internal Auditing in State Agencies

The study cited contains a fairly extensive description of the current status of state internal auditing, but a few points need to be cited here to form the basis of the recommendations we'll set forth.

First, out of all of the departments and agencies of state government, only 115 of them were reported to have internal auditors whose responsibility could be defined as that of conducting an independent appraisal of (1) financial records and controls, (2) the efficiency of operations, and/or (3) the effectiveness of programs. When questionnaires were sent to the internal auditor and the agency head of each of these 115 agencies, and when personal visits and telephone interviews were made to expand the survey and confirm the questionnaire results, it was discovered that a large number of these 115 agencies had a person with the title of internal auditor but whose duties were something other than those described above. In short, very few agencies of state governments in this country currently have an internal audit staff or program.

Yet, in spite of the relative infrequency with which such staffs and programs are found today, the sentiment expressed by administrators, legislators, and chief state auditors overwhelmingly supported such programs as being very important to efficiency and effectiveness in state programs.

The Challenge and Opportunity to The Institute

To one who is converted to the positive benefits of good internal auditing it should not be difficult to understand the urgency of the challenge nor the magnitude of the opportunity to the membership of The Institute, collectively or individually, to render a valuable public service by promoting the establishment of internal audit programs in virtually all state agencies. Not only must such programs exist; they must also be of professional quality. In other words, they must be staffed with qualified personnel, be given sufficient independence and authority to enable them to conduct meaningful evaluations, and be supported financially and otherwise in the performance of their duties.

The Institute and its members can do much to bring about improvements in these areas. A few possibilities are suggested in the following paragraphs.

The Institute and its chapters must support substantive research focusing on the special problems of evaluation and control in government. The study sponsored by the Washington Chapter is an example of what can be done, but it is only a small beginning in what should be a much greater involvement in research in public-sector internal auditing.

The Institute and its chapters should be especially alert to opportunities to have input to efforts of constitutional revision and government reorganization so that appropriate language can be incorporated into the resulting documents to provide for internal audit and review programs in all state agencies. Similarly, efforts should be made to encourage these provisions in bills to create new programs and/or organizational units in state government.

A greater effort should be made to invite to membership in The Institute and its chapters all internal auditors and their staffs now found in state agencies. Moreover, as membership alone is not enough, special attention should be given to providing appropriate professional development programs and seminars of particular relevance and interest to these auditors.

The Institute and its chapters should work more closely with government officials in helping to establish standards of competence for classification as internal auditors in state agencies and for promoting a sufficiently high classification structure to attract qualified and dedicated persons to these positions.

The members of The Institute should more actively support public officials who have a genuine interest in improving financial management. Such support includes not only working for their election or appointment but also working closely with them as they seek to establish and strengthen sound internal audit programs and other elements of good operational control.

The literature of the association should include a wider discussion of topics relevant to internal auditing in government. Such discussions will not only help the members of the association become more aware of the opportunities and challenges in the public sector but will also encourage a greater participation of public-sector auditors in The Institute's programs and activities.

The Institute should develop and promulgate appropriate statements of principles and standards covering internal audit work in government. One example of this type of statement would be a response to the statement entitled *Standards for Audit of Governmental Organizations, Programs, Activities, and Functions,* recently issued by the U. S. Comptroller General. Another would be to address the question of the role of the internal auditor in satisfying grant requirements under federal assistance programs to state and local government.

Finally, The Institute could render a valuable service by preparing position papers on controversial issues involving internal auditing in government agencies and by giving expert testimony on such matters before legislative committees and special commissions whose responsibility includes a study of these matters.

In short, then, if we can take a creative and imaginative approach to meeting this challenge, we will find many opportunities to promote more and better internal audits in state agencies. Let us seize our opportunity and meet the challenge before us. In so doing all the world will know this association renders a valuable public service in promoting improved government and better public service.

Operational Auditing in Georgia

Ernest B. Davis

The Internal Auditor May/June 1974

The operational audit was initiated in Georgia during 1971 as a result of a short paragraph in the annual "Appropriation Act," which says: "From the above amount the sum of $150,000 is committed for the employment of ten performance auditors and related costs to initiate the Performance Audit Program."

Actually Georgia statutes have provided for audits in more depth than post-financial from 1923 on, as the following excerpt from the "Department of Audits Act" shows:

> "To prepare annual and whenever required, special reports to the Governor and the General Assembly, showing the general financial operation and *management* of each State department, institution, agency, commission and bureau, and whether or not the same is being handled in an *efficient* and *economical* manner, and calling special attention to any excessive cost of operation or maintenance, and excessive expense, and any excessive price paid for goods, supplies or labor by any such department, institution, agency, etc."

Other sections of the same Act provided that certain audits had to be performed each year, published and in the hands of the Legislature when they convened in January. Approximately 416 financial audits (State Agencies, Universities, Colleges, and Boards of Education) are in this category. This established that it would be impractical to attempt performance audits in conjunction with post-financial audits.

SEPARATE STAFF DEVELOPED

From this premise was developed a separate staff to comply with Legislative intent, for "Operational Audits" on facilities and programs.

It was soon apparent that without the financial audit component included, staff other than financial auditors might well add a desirable dimension. Accordingly recruiting was broadened to include management and business administration majors with accounting, personnel and statistical backgrounds. The decision was made to classify all staff members as management analysts rather than auditors. To some extent this has alleviated the problem of competency when treading on sacred ground in professional program areas. This has been the biggest single obstacle to overcome as professional personnel believe all auditors belong with financial records and not program results.

REPORT FORMAT DESIGNED TO EDUCATE READER

Report format was designed to fulfill the primary purposes of educating the reader or legislator as to what was actually being accomplished at the facility or in the program and to present to middle management and top management, documentation of its deficiencies and accomplishments. Narrative reports are rendered on each examination, with presentation arranged on each section or subject to provide a description of what has been proposed by the agency or program administrator as regular operating procedure, what in fact is happening (findings), and a recommendation for improvement, if justified.

Every attempt is made to be objective and constructive in any criticism. Quantitative analysis and statistical comparisons in professional areas are presented for reader review without attempt to judge quality or results.

BASIC PREMISE: Economical, Efficient Operation Equals Best Results Obtainable

This approach permits the evaluation of economy and efficiency to the extent that inadequacies in management, operating procedures and lack of documentation must be detrimental. Program results or effectiveness are extremely difficult to measure in the absence of valid criteria. One must be very cautious in using standards established under ideal or sterile conditions. It is believed that each set of results being measured is individual and the proper viewpoint is that if the operation is economical and efficient the results will be as effective as could be expected under the circumstances. If the emphasis in operational auditing is placed on determining the weaknesses in management, operating procedures and documentation, the correction of these elements will lead to more efficient and effective programs which, in the final analysis, will provide the necessary criteria for standards of performance.

It Works In Georgia!

Admittedly the above approach may not be entirely consistent with the volumes of data now available on performance, program and operational auditing; however, it has been accepted and is working in state government in Georgia. To date some eighteen facilities and seven program audits have been performed with satisfying results.

The Importance of Internal Auditing In Counties and Municipalities

Dr. Meyer Drucker, CPA

The Internal Auditor Nov./Dec. 1973

All levels of government are faced with serious financing problems. Local governments probably have the most serious funding problems because the requests for services from its constituencies are exceeding its sources of funds. Presently, independent appraisal activity within cities and counties in the U. S. and Canada for the review of accounting, financial and management operations is in its infancy. These governments should be able to improve their operating efficiencies through proper use of internal auditing just as private companies have long used this vehicle for improving operations.

Government Units Should Justify Existence

The profit motive is lacking as a measure of operating efficiency in the governmental environment. The taxpayer, the "owner" of the governmental unit, often cannot understand the published financial reports because of antiquated legal requirements. Therefore, the average taxpayer must rely on gossip or oratory from politicians for information. Because of this vital point, governmental units should justify their existence on the basis of efficiency of operations as well as upon the needs of society. The need for internal review within the governmental environment is, therefore, probably even more vital than for the profit-oriented organization.

Independence of Internal Auditors Increases Value

Internal auditors, who are truly independent from operations and have the grasp of an organization's financial records, can provide invaluable assistance to politicians and administrators because they are aware of the full range of problems facing the reviewed activity. Therefore, it is essential that the internal auditing function be responsible to an officer whose authority is sufficient to assure (a) a broad range of coverage will be made and (b) effective action will be taken on the audit recommendations.

Local governments lag far behind private industry and the Federal Government in using internal auditing as a tool for controlling operations. As a minimum, the legislative body should receive a summary of the audit findings. Reactions and comments to the detailed reports should be required from the affected departments.

Where internal auditing is used in local governments, it is often not sufficiently independent of the reviewed activities in order to be of service to municipal officials. To insure the optimum use of internal auditing, the chief auditor should be appointed by and report to the legislative body.

New Era Dawning

On the brighter side, a few local governments are beginning to realize the value of this important tool and are establishing internal auditing departments for the first time. In addition, many existing departments are being strengthened.

Progressive Auditing in King County

Lloyd F. Hara

The Internal Auditor Nov./Dec. 1972

Until recently, the Auditor's Section in King County (Seattle, Wash.) had the traditional image of verification of revenue receipts against treasurer's deposit slips, checking expenditure vouchers against budget codes, reviewing payroll and other transactions for proper coding, etc. Today in King County auditing includes (1) legal or compliance auditing, (2) fiscal auditing, and (3) management, operational or performance auditing. The Internal auditor performs all forms of audits so that management is aware that sound financial practices are being followed, proper stewardship of funds is maintained, legal mandates and legislative intent are followed, and overall efficiency, effectiveness and economy are practiced in administration of programs.

In King County, the Auditor's Office has set a goal:

> "To promote greater economy, effectiveness, and efficiency in King County Government by utilization of sound management principles, and to maintain a high level of public confidence in their public officials to deliver desired and needed services."

The internal auditor holds a staff position. He advises and offers recommendations. He is *not* a line officer. He reviews programs, but does not run them. The internal audit system offers (1) additional management *information,* (2) *alternatives,* (3) *objectivity,* (4) bridge from *inter-office communication,* and (5) *expertise* not normally found in the small organization.

Relationship Between Internal and External Auditors

The relationship between internal and external audits can vary substantially, depending on the size of organization and legal requirements. Generally the internal audit function is part of the management process and is reviewed by the external auditor. There are areas of mutual interest between the internal and external auditor. The external auditor reviews working papers of the internal auditor to gain information during his examination and to gauge the effectiveness of the internal audit function. Aside from analyzing financial statements, the external auditor makes recommendations to improve the operation of the organization including the internal auditor.

In King County, audits are conducted covering the period since the last audit. We do not confine ourselves to calendar or fiscal years. The external auditor, the State Auditor's Office, confines itself to fiscal years (and is limited by law to review only the fiscal and legal compliance matters) and performs the certified audit. Because of the differences in audit function, the two offices work closely together, resulting in a minimum of duplication.

To Whom Should the Auditor Report

Some believe the auditor must be elected to maintain true *independence.* Others feel the auditor should be appointed by the chief executive officer or should be appointed by legislature or council so as to truly appraise conditions without pressures from politicians or from management. Also, the auditor must command a position of *sufficient rank* to have easy access to key decision-makers and not get lost in the layers of the bureaucracy.

The King County auditor is a charter officer established within the legislative branch. The auditor cannot engage in partisan politics and is appointed by the County Council for a fixed term of office. The auditor can be removed only for just cause of misfeasance or malfeasance of office by a two-thirds vote of the legislative body. The charter also states the auditor will advise the chief executive on accounting and fiscal matters. To fulfill this advisory role, the auditor meets every two weeks with the county executive to discuss matters of mutual interest or concern.

A Strategy to Establish the Internal Auditor Office

Developing *credibility* is the first critical step to becoming effective. Most organizations and managers tend to be defensive or even hostile when an outsider questions their modus operandi. Many governmental managers have never been scrutinized in this fashion before, unlike the manager in private industry who welcomes assistance to improve his profit and loss statement.

It is tactically prudent to select for the first audits departments with a reputation of being poorly administered and mismanaged. The auditor can readily offer recommendations to top management without dangerous repercussions from those departments under audit investigation. In most cases, many of the auditor accommodations can be implemented immediately whereby both top management and the auditors can see concrete results from the audit.

Sufficient time and care should be spent to thoroughly document and present audit findings. Usually the auditor will come under heavy questioning to prove his professional judgment and substantiate his findings. The total process from planning the audit to writing the report requires the close attention of everyone on the audit.

In King County the auditor has purposely waited until the second and third years to prove his capability and credibility before attacking the "sacred cows." He has used an approach that allowed him to early gain easy access into an organization, to make concrete recommendations without strong opposition and gain time to perfect our system of audit.

Staff members should be generalists, knowledgeable in many phases of management and able to analyze and evaluate operations at all levels of administration. They should have technical expertise in operations research, statistical sampling, economic analysis and industrial engineering techniques, computer science, management science and other management skills. Obviously it is the unusual individual who is thoroughly knowledgeable in all these modern management tools, but all must be familiar enough with such tools to be able to apply them later if given minimal training.

Establishing an Internal Audit Function in County Government

Thomas J. Falstad

The Internal Auditor May/June 1973

The internal audit function at Hennepin County, Minn., is relatively new, only two years old. Encountered were certain inherent differences (when compared to the private sector) that affected the plan for establishing an internal audit organization.

Hennepin County includes the City of Minneapolis and serves one million people. The county government includes 35 departments employing over 5,000 people, and it has an operating budget of approximately $230 million. Operations include a general hospital, libraries, a district and municipal court system, a highway department, welfare department, police and many other activities normally carried out by a county government.

The county has many of the basic characteristics of any organization, and consequently its financial and management information reporting system are similar in many respects. The accounting system is designed to provide management and operating personnel with sound financial information upon which to make operating decisions, and to assist in carrying out stewardship responsibilities. County objectives include providing a high level of service to those people that must be served in an economical and effective manner. These objectives are no different than any profit-oriented organization. The basic difference inherent in county government that affects internal audit is not the basic objective but the priorities and relative emphases placed thereon, and the wide range of the services rendered.

Hennepin County government is responsible for administering a wide variety of diverse services. Many of the operating (and audit problems) inherent in a 400-bed general hospital are foreign to a large public works program, just as a county-wide library system's activities are largely unrelated to a welfare department's activities. Since the county is not competing with other organizations and its services are not paid by those directly benefited by them, it is relatively difficult to evaluate the effectiveness of programs which would, in turn, help to determine the allocation of limited resources. The lack of a profit motive tends to result in a more program-oriented management than cost-oriented (which it is believed is desirable as long as the county maintains a satisfactory level of "economy" consciousness). This philosophy had resulted in a very cash-oriented, antiquated accounting system that had never been substantially modified up to one year ago.

The county's sources of revenue are as diverse as its operations. Recently, it has depended on relatively less property tax revenues and is sharing the cost of more of its activities with the federal government through such means as federal LEAA grants, federal revenue sharing, county-wide overhead cost absorbtion of federally assisted programs and various expanded welfare programs. This change in financial arrangements means that, in addition to a complex variety of legal and statutory requirements, the county must conform to a wide range of federal/state reporting requirements. A result is that it is continually being audited by a large number of federal and state audit agencies in addition to the State Public Examiner's office and the county's own independent public accountants.

In order to carry out an effective internal audit function designed to perform financial, compliance and operational audits, it was concluded that initially, a relatively small, highly skilled staff would be the most productive. Because of the diversity of operations, an effective auditor must be able to quickly grasp the operating characteristics and recognize potential problem areas of the activity subject to audit.

The county now has a small but highly skilled audit staff. Three of the present staff members are certified public accountants and have broad experience in public accounting. The core of the staff, because of its experience and heavy commercial audit background, has given a fresh business approach to auditing a governmental entity; a factor that it was felt was particularly important during the formative stages of the function.

Although the staff is involved in detail verification of invoices, examination of warrants, confirmation and other standard audit procedures, emphasis has been given to working closely with large county departments (such as Welfare and the General Hospital) particularly in developing adequate financial/accounting controls and the procedures necessary to monitor these controls. Internal audit then audits the operating department's monitoring process to insure that the control function is being carried out effectively. The objectives have been to insure the procedures were adequate when originally established and that the procedures are actually being followed. Since most of the county operations are also subject to several non-county audit agencies as discussed, the audit staff works closely with them to coordinate all audit activities so as to insure proper audit coverage.

This approach used by the Internal Audit Department has provided much flexibility. It gives the opportunity to concentrate on other, sometimes more productive activities, particularly operational auditing. Because of the service oriented, non-competitive nature of the county's operations, a great deal of professional judgment has to be exercised in order to make a useful evaluation of services the county renders. In addition, the staff is continually alert to ways of maximizing present and potential, non-property tax revenue sources.

Although the audit activity is still developing, the staff has been able to demonstrate to the County Board of Commissioners and Administration that a separate internal audit staff in a county government of this size is not only economically feasible, but highly desirable.

The county has, in recent years, become heavily involved in "sponsoring" or underwriting numerous small non-county organizations funded by federal law enforcement grants. Included in the county's responsibilities are fiscal and program direction over the agencies to insure services are rendered in accordance with federal grant regulations.

In our review, we found a great diversity in the adequacy and uniformity of policies and procedures followed by individual operating agencies. In addition, the county had little centralized control over the operations of these agencies. In some instances it was found that the agencies' operations were duplicating the services of both county departments as well as other non-county agencies.

As a result of our review, we recommended that, (1) financial and program controls be centralized and made uniform to all agencies to the extent practical; and (2) to insure proper financial and accounting controls are maintained, require that the basic accounting functions (payroll preparation, preparation of budget control/financial reports) be done by the county accounting system.

As a result, a manual was developed that incorporated these recommendations. The agencies rely upon the county for financial and certain operational expertise. Because of the county's fully computerized accounting system, we have been able to provide the necessary assistance at no additional cost. The agency also has available to it the county's financial and program expertise, and the county has been able to fulfill its responsibilities under federal grant regulations.

Historically the county had required cumbersome expenditure review requirements. The extensive time delay resulted in the loss of cash discounts and incurred additional costs from suppliers to compensate for these delays.

Our review of the entire expenditure process disclosed that, in addition to payment approvals normally followed by governmental entities, our process required review and approval by the county attorney's office and county purchasing department. This resulted in a great amount of unnecessary duplication of effort. Because of workload requirements and lack of clarity as to exactly what their reviews were to include, additional delays of up to two weeks were noted.

We recommended that expenditure procedures be modified to eliminate reviews by these two departments. The result is that payment delays have been significantly reduced and clerical time has been saved.

Performance Auditing and the Governmental Accounting Course

James M. Williams, CPA

The Internal Auditor July/Aug. 1974

The governmental accounting course in the collegiate curriculum has often been criticized for its traditional approach.

The available governmental texts have emphasized the fiscal aspects of fund accounting and budgetary control for state and local governments as recommended by the National Committee on Governmental Accounting. Understandably, this approach has generated little enthusiasm for the course.

With the desire to incorporate the expanding scope of and the new material in commercial accounting into the curriculum, many academicians have even questioned the desirability of a governmental course.

Ironically, this reaction to the governmental course is coming at the very time when efforts to improve all aspects of governmental financial management are at their peak and when more contributions are being made to governmental accounting literature than ever before.

The task is to make the governmental accounting course more challenging.

The course should place a greater emphasis on managerial information and decision making. Expired costs or expenses should be determined in the same way as commercial accounting and should be related to programs and to quantitative measures of accomplishment of objectives.

This information is essential in the planning, management and control, and evaluation of governmental programs. This material would emphasize the challenge facing governmental accounting to improve performance in addition to the fiscal responsibilities. Another logical topic for inclusion in this expanded governmental accounting course is performance auditing, since it builds on a managerial orientation.

Performance Auditing Advocated

The term "performance auditing" is an expanded concept of governmental audit responsibility that has been advocated under a variety of different names. Lennis M. Knighton offers a reconciliation of audit concepts beyond the financial audit. With the related elements presented in brackets, Knighton offers the following definition of the performance audit:

> "an examination of records and other evidence to support an appraisal or evaluation of the efficiency of government operations [operational audit], the effectiveness of government programs [program audit], and the faithfulness of responsible administrators to adhere to juridical requirements and administrative policies pertaining to their programs and organizations [compliance audit]."[1]

Performance auditing has received a significant boost from the publication of the GAO Audit Standards.[2] Since their publication, the Audit Standards have received wide exposure in the accounting periodicals, including *The Internal Auditor*.[3] Although the impetus for the development of the standards was largely to facilitate federal agency acceptance of the audits of federally assisted programs, the standards are intended to apply to audits of all government levels and other types of audits.

The performance auditing aspects are evidenced by the full scope of the following three elements embodied in the Audit Standards (Knighton's corresponding elements are presented in brackets):

(1) *financial and compliance* — an examination of financial transactions, accounts, and reports, including an evaluation of compliance with applicable laws and regulations [compliance audit];

(2) *economy and efficiency* — a review of the efficiency and economy in the use of resources [operational audit]; and

(3) *program results* — a review to determine whether desired results are effectively achieved [program audit].[4]

The Logical Place for Performance Auditing

The governmental accounting course is the logical place in the accounting curriculum for performance auditing. The auditing course has been almost exclusively limited to commercial financing auditing. With the current developments and pronouncements in commercial auditing, the scope of the auditing course will likely remain unchanged. On the other hand, governmental financial auditing has always been covered in the governmental accounting texts. This material should be expanded to include performance auditing.

Three new governmental accounting texts are coming out in the near future. Hopefully, they will contain extensive coverage of the Audit Standards and performance auditing. In the long run, including this material in the texts will be the best way to assure adequate coverage in the governmental course. In the short run, the Audit Standards are available at the reasonable cost of sixty-five cents. Also, numerous articles are available for assignment on different aspects of performance auditing (particularly in *The Internal Auditor, The Federal Accountant,* and *The Journal of Accountancy).*

Challenging Career Opportunity

Including performance auditing in the governmental course can reveal a challenging career opportunity to students who are already interested in the public sector. By attracting more qualified students into performance auditing, the profession can expand its capacity to conduct these audits. This increased capability will yield the benefit of improved performance of government programs.

---

[1]*Lennis M. Knighton, "An Integrated Framework for Conceptualizing Alternative Ap*proaches to State Audit Programs," *The Federal Accountant,* XX (March, 1971), pp. 10-11.

[2]U.S. General Accounting Office, *Standards for Audit of Governmental Organizations, Programs, Activities & Functions* (Washington: U.S. Government Printing Office, 1973), 54 pp.

[3]See especially Mortimer A. Dittenhofer, "The New Audit Standards and Internal Auditing," *The Internal Auditor,* XXXI (January/February, 1974), pp. 10-12, 14-23.

[4]U.S. General Accounting Office, *op. cit.,* pp. 2 and 6.

Is Auditing a *Sine Qua Non* in The Management Process?

Dr. William L. Campfield, CPA

The Internal Auditor Sept./Oct. 1973

Is Auditing a *Sine Qua Non* in the Management Process? The above pretentious question could just as easily have been reworded into "Are auditors getting too big for their britches?" By putting the question this way, we pose the overriding query of why auditors believe they have a foundation for considering themselves the right people to assess the effectiveness of managers and the management process.

We could if we wished peremptorily dismiss all of the alternative questions with one whimsical observation and two serious ones, namely:

–There are only two kinds of people in the world – the *qualified* (auditors) and the *unqualified* – and the qualified determine which is which.

–The auditor as we have conventionally known him has been historically recognized as expert in examining accounting controls, personnel controls, production cost controls, etc., etc. Consequently, he has by sheer weight of experience and acceptance 'earned' the role of management controls evaluator.

–Somewhat akin to the sense of the Rheingold commercial, auditors 'must be doing something right' since so many of them are being retained in both the private and the public sectors to help responsible managements achieve economy, efficiency and effectiveness in their planning and operations.

As partial support for this assertion note that a not-too-long-ago survey of 114 corporations revealed among other things:

- 72% of the entities have a director of auditing whose position is at the corporate level,
- 83% of the entities have audit staffs performing what is now known as management auditing, and
- over a third of the surveyed entities stated that substantial cost savings had been achieved through follow-up and corrective action taken as a result of management audit findings and recommendations.[1] An earlier study of 45 Federal departments and agencies showed that 78% of these organizations had audit organizational units doing management audits.[2]

With evidence such as the above to bulwark us, let us now establish a rationale for what the auditor needs to know and do in order to

---

[1]Choi, Jong T., "Operational Auditing - Part 1," *The Internal Auditor,* March/April, 1971.

[2]*Internal Auditing – Review and Appraisal in the Federal Government* – Research Bulletin No. 2, Federal Government Accountants Association, Washington, D. C., 1972, p. 19.

serve as a top counsel to managements.

Content of the Knowledge/ Proficiency Role of the Auditor

Perhaps we can best visualize the integrated content of the management auditor's knowledge/skill as a pyramid in which:

—*The foundation* of the structure represents the auditor's knowledge, judgment and applied techniques in examining and analyzing accounting and related informational flows and events.

—*Each ascending* tier of the structure represents the auditor's additional knowledge and skill in reviewing and appraising important non-accounting aspects of an entity's activities, such as: project planning, flexible budgets, engineered performance standards, personnel administration, and so on.

—*The pinnacle* of the structure represents the auditor's unified knowledge, skills, judgment and, most importantly, his perspective regarding the goals, the programs and the long-range mission outputs of the entity about which he renders opinions and advice.

An Indispensable Part of Management Process

If we were to seek empiric support for our belief that a management-oriented auditor is indeed an indispensable part of the management process, we would search for and, likely find, assurance that the auditor has system and methodology that:

—Furnishes him with sufficient information about an entity's policies, structure, programs and network of management controls to enable him to proceed with representative, economical and substantive examination and testing of actual operations.

—Permits him to ascertain first-hand whether the entity's system of planning and performance controls do in fact operate as prescribed.

—Results in his deriving a balanced evaluation of an entity's operations which can be understandingly communicated to and is acceptable by, the entity's management as a basis for improving future planning and performance.

Two-Way Communicator

Still another way to look at the management auditor's purview and competence is to view him as an entity's two-way communicator throughout the entity:

—In the *downward flow* process, i.e., from top management to middle management to supervisory management to front-line employee, we may envision the auditor as an individual who ascertains whether messages on the important policies and plans get to the people responsible for action in sufficient time and detail for required action. As a corollary, we can sense the auditor ascertaining (and assisting where relevant) whether there is a reasonable meeting of the minds all the way down as to the meaning of the management messages.

—In the *upward flow process,* i.e., from front-line operations centers up through line, staff and other levels to the very top, we may profile the auditor ascertaining whether data needed for planning and control purposes is being disseminated timely, and whether there has been a 'siphoning off' or dilution of data at subordinate levels during the upward flow.

To aid and abet his communication role, the auditor could, during his preliminary surveying work or testing of the *'prima facies'* of an entity, flow chart the downward movement of policy statements, directives, etc. He could also chart the upward flow of plans, programs, schedules, reports, directives, etc. The budget formulation and approval flows is an excellent example of policy/activity flow that might be examined by an auditor in order to test the adequacy of communications in an entity.

Dedicated to 'Flushing' Out the Inhibitors

A final way to think about the auditor's managerial usefulness is to think of him as constantly dedicated to the proposition of helping a management 'flush' out the profit-inhibitors or the inhibitors to planned output. The auditor might, without inordinate effort, uncover plans and programs that are too ambitious in light of known limitations on input resources. Or, he might find programs too inflexibly drawn to permit adjustment to real life constraints. For example, there have been cases of Federal grants to educational institutions to correct basic reading and writing deficiencies in children in which the amount of resources was too small, and the time limits for accomplishment too short, to correct hard core deficiencies.

It is axiomatic that the degree to which an entity turns out goods and services in accordance with plans turns on how well employees throughout the entity accept and adhere to that entity's goals, programs, performance-standards and performance-rewards systems. The proficient and perceptive auditor can help all levels of people in the entity by pointing up dispassionately those actions/reactions that inhibit outputs or profits, as the case may be.

Basic Purpose to Help Find 'Best Ways'

I have tried to say simply that the basic purpose of management auditing is to help entity managements find 'best ways' to manage their entities.

The auditor's unending search for better, less costly and more effective ways of doing things can make him a vital force in the management of any entity that has the problem of getting the best return from scarce resources.

5
scope of operational audit

Independence has long been termed by many as the most essential audit standard. This is true of the AICPA standards that have been in effect for many years and of the GAO standards, issued in 1972. Without independence an audit is nothing more than an in-depth study. However, the GAO standard that has had the greatest impact on the audit community is the one describing scope. This standard was taken from internal auditing as practiced in industry and government, especially by auditors from the GAO and other agencies practicing progressive auditing.

The traditional audit was concerned with financial operations. Auditors reviewed financial transactions and related processes in depth to determine the validity of financial reports and statements, the existence of internal controls, and the safeguarding of organizational assets. The detection of clerical inaccuracy was a by-product and the exposure of fraud, embezzlement, and other types of malfeasance — although not specific objectives — became serendipitous output. Later, the determination that financial operations be conducted faithfully, efficiently, and effectively was identified as a basic objective. Compliance with procedures and statutes was also reviewed in the process of determining validity and reliability of financial aspects.

Two basic factors have contributed to the expanded scope of auditing in government. First, government has grown in size and complexity. Second, auditors, through their examination and evaluation of financial controls, have developed skills useful in the evaluation of management. A third probable factor was an environment ready for operational auditing — an environment where resources were becoming scarce and where management was becoming increasingly aware of its basic accountability for their use. Obviously, this environment contained scattered pockets of resistance. Overall, however, the setting was favorable.

First, expansion came into the area of determining compliance with policy, plans, statutes, and regulations. The auditor's objective was to determine that laws and regulations were considered in the promulgation of plans and policy; that controls were in use to assure compliance; and that requirements being complied with were reasonable, efficient, and effective. There was a very close relationship of compliance auditing with financial auditing because noncompliance in many cases resulted in financial sanctions or payback.

The second area of expansion was in the field of operational or management auditing. This activity was intended to provide managers at all levels, legislatures, and the public with information on how efficiently resources were being employed and consumed. If the auditee had a system of planning and controls to supply this information, the auditor tested the system. If no system existed, the auditor, with the auditee, established an ad hoc control system of standards, feedback, and evaluation in order to make constructive recommendations based on the system results.

Finally, the scope of the operational audit was extended into the area of effectiveness or program-results auditing. This segment of the audit determined how effectively the auditee was achieving goals and objectives. As in efficiency auditing, if a control system was in operation, it was tested. If there was no control system, a substitute process was developed to determine effectiveness and to make recommendations for improvements.

The complete scope of the audit sounds like a tall order. In effect, only those segments where potential benefits exceed cost by a predetermined magnitude are to be completed. This expansion of scope is really what set operational auditing apart from the financial audit. The need was great, for public resources were — and are — at a premium. And efficiency and effectiveness were — and are — essential.

The first section of this chapter is short. It is an article on the audit of financial controls, insuring financial integrity. The author, John P. Callahan, is director of the Division of State Auditing, New Jersey.

The second part deals with the first segment of expanded scope, compliance auditing. John P. Proctor, state auditor of Colorado, describes the concept of compliance auditing in a general sense. John J. Lordan, Office of Management and Budget, expands on the authoritative criteria essential to the compliance audit. W. B. Bolton, Canadian government, examines the auditing of financial compliance areas in government as apart from operational compliance. Gerald J. Lonergan, county auditor of San Diego County, California, identifies the close relationship between compliance auditing and the management audit. The section concludes with a case study in compliance auditing by Richard E. Brown and Jeffrey H. Brewer, director and project manager respectively, of the Kansas legislative audit operation.

The third part of this chapter covers management or efficiency audits. The first article by Richard J. Griffin, assistant comptroller for auditing, U.S. Atomic Energy Commission (now Energy Research and Development Agency), describes the functional auditing developed by that agency as an innovation in 1954. Lloyd F. Hara, auditor of King County, Washington, tells how to perform economy and efficiency audits in local governments and Martin Ives, CPA, former New York State deputy comptroller and now deputy comptroller of New York City, proves how efficiency audits can determine the allocation of resources in carrying out government programs.

Effectiveness or program-results audits make up the fourth section. John W. Fawsett, associate director of the U.S. Army Audit Agency, explores the evaluation of effectiveness and the impact of improvements in one system on the operation of other systems. Dr. C. David Baron, Arizona State University, identifies the effectiveness audit as an integral part of periodic management review and cites its benefits. Dr. Meyer Drucker, University of South Carolina, discusses the effectiveness audit and its benefits to local governments.

The section concludes with an article by Dr. Lennis M. Knighton, auditor general of Utah. Dr. Knighton focuses on three questions: (1) What was accomplished? (2) Was the program successful? (3) Is there an adequate and appropriate control system? Dr. Knighton concludes by explaining the basis of evaluation and the potential benefits of the audit.

A final section consists of an article on measuring employee perceptions as a part of management auditing. The objective of this audit is to improve the use of human resources. This article by Guy K. Zimmerman, Office of Internal Audit, U.S. Department of Labor, is based on a 100-item questionnaire that also served effectively as a part of the preliminary audit survey.

Audit of Financial Controls

John P. Callahan

The Internal Auditor June 1976

In reflecting on the history of the U.S. government, we can attest to shifts of emphasis in the way the public sees government. For example, immediately after the Russians launched their sputnik into outer space, there was a great sentiment for a similar feat by this country. This, in turn, saw a demand for the involvement of governmental resources and public funds into education—primarily the technical field.

Today with dramatic fiscal crises, both at the national and local level, the sentiment is for greater accountability by governmental officials; and as some refer to it, "this may be the golden age for the auditor." Therefore, our responsibility as auditors in providing this test of accountability is probably seen by many as meeting government's greatest immediate need in terms of public confidence.

In New Jersey, the actual performance of our audits encompasses a critical review of an agency's financial controls to insure that proper fiscal integrity is maintained on an ongoing basis. With the growth of government at all levels—in terms of complexity, scope, and cost—there has been a corresponding increase in the need for effective financial controls. This has generated formidable problems in auditing the massive and complex data which have proliferated. These problems have demanded quick response and innovation on the part of the auditing community. In New Jersey, for example, in 1971, the auditing function was completely revamped to meet emerging needs. From a limited type of revenue audit, the Legislative Office of Fiscal Affairs now has the complete overview capability to monitor financial control through the planning (budgetary), doing (financial and compliance), and reviewing (program evaluation) processes which make up the fiscal control system.

Controls Are Basic to Management

However, it may be well to discuss the concept of controls in general at this point. Controls are basic to every type of activity in management. For the small organization, controls are rather simple and straightforward. However, as organizations grow, they are required to use more formal control procedures to insure that employees' actions are consistent with management's intent and objectives. When we refer to the audit of financial controls, we include accounting controls, administrative controls, and internal controls. As governmental accounting systems advance from the bookkeeping-tabulating equipment to computers, the process becomes highly systematized; therefore, the audits are much more complex. Thus, it is essential that the accounting system have built-in self-checking and error-detection routines for discipline and adherence to systematized requirements or documentation and the like.

Our audit program in New Jersey is probably not greatly different from that used by most state auditors and private accountants in the area of auditing financial and internal controls. The rationale for the audit is threefold:

(1) It determines the amount of specific testing necessary to complete the job in an efficient manner, insuring results which are both valid and applicable.

(2) It provides the public with accountability.

(3) It provides verification to management that the data being generated are accurate, thus leading to proper action.

Auditing Financial Controls

The actual performance of an audit of financial controls incorporates the use of many tools such as questionnaires, observations, interviews, and testing. In addition, we include relatively newer techniques such as flowcharting and discovery sampling. While the professional auditor will begin each assignment with a general plan of action and will incorporate some combination of these tools and others at his disposal, it is necessary that he be flexible enough to alter his strategy where conditions warrant changes. Each program to be audited presents the auditor with a unique set of strengths and weaknesses. The skilled auditor will utilize the resources at hand to identify existing weaknesses and to formulate plans to correct its deficiencies.

There is always the argument relative to the cost of providing sound financial controls, but we probably need only to look to New York City to see what the true cost of a lack of adequate budgetary and financial controls can be. Certainly, there were many factors in the New York City financial crises; but there seems to be no question that the lack of adequate financial controls aggravated the problem and precipitated charges of "accounting and budget gimmickry" of city officials. Public accountability and confidence ebbed as repercussions of New York reverberated throughout the country into the financial markets themselves.

In our audits of 95% of state government during the past three years, we have found that our recommendations for enhancing or increasing controls have been well accepted. This accomplishment has been assisted by an effective audit compliance program. However, since such controls cost time and money, there is always an economic judgment by the executive management as to whether a further degree of assurance is worth the cost of providing it. Therefore, in our recommendations, we attempt to recommend only those improvements in controls which we feel are essential to the proper functioning of the agency and which are both technically and economically feasible.

Age of Accountability Means Greater Audit Responsibility

In summary, the "age of accountability" has placed added responsibility on the auditor for the establishment and maintenance of a proper system of financial control at every level of government operation. Indeed, the audit itself is a control designed to insure that all other controls are working. No longer can we satisfy ourselves as to the adequacy of financial control and feel we have done our job. We must constantly strive to strengthen them if we are to restore and maintain the public confidence. This will challenge the auditors' skills not only in identifying weaknesses in financial controls and offering recommendations for improvement but in taking an active role in seeing to it that these recommendations are implemented. The future will be challenging, indeed, for the auditor. By his training, independence, and objectivity, he or she is in a unique position to make a positive contribution to strengthening financial controls over public funds. This is not only desirable, but it is essential if the democratic form of government which includes "checks and balances" is to thrive.

Compliance Auditing

John P. Proctor, CPA

The Internal Auditor Jan./Feb. 1975

The term "compliance auditing" is easily defined; but its connotation is often bandied, distorted, and misunderstood. Consequently, there is a need for greater understanding of the compliance audit function and its overall relationship within the total auditing spectrum. With greater understanding of the interdependency between compliance, financial, and performance auditing, both program administrators and auditors will make a significant contribution to the improvement of government services.

The compliance audit should be an integral part of financial and operational or performance audits and should not generally be considered as a separate examination. Basically, this is due to the nature of compliance audits since most aspects of these examinations overlap with financial and performance auditing. This view of compliance auditing is not always used by members of our profession. It is increasingly being used in a manner so as to imply that everyone understands and agrees that compliance auditing is a separate and distinct entity.

Theoretical and Actual Interdependency

There is a theoretical and actual interdependency between compliance auditing and financial and performance auditing. Some of this interdependency may be seen from the usual definition for compliance auditing. This definition states that a compliance audit is a review of agency actions for determining compliance with legal and regulatory requirements. However, it is also true that a financial audit entails determining compliance with legal requirements. For example, in a financial audit, the auditor determines whether the agency maintained its spending within limits appropriated by the legislative body. Clearly, this audit action is for the purpose of determining, as stated in the above definition, compliance with legal requirements.

Additional insight to the relationship between compliance, financial, and performance auditing will be gained by examining the two basic purposes of compliance auditing. The following statement from the GAO publication entitled *Standards for Audit of Governmental Organizations, Programs, Activities and Functions* addresses the first reason for compliance auditing:

"In governmental auditing, compliance with pertinent laws and regulations is particularly significant because government organizations, functions, programs, or activities are creatures of law and have more specific rules and regulations than are usually applicable to private organizations."

This explanation as to the purpose of compliance auditing is based upon the conceptual control philosophy of governmental accounting, reporting, and auditing as distinguished from private profit-orientated enterprises. Since there is no profit objective through which the discharge of governmental administrators' responsibility may be evaluated, accountants have turned to the concept of "dollar accountability."

Certain techniques, like fund accounting and appropriation-budget control, are used by accountants to meet their responsibility in maintaining dollar accountability. Because these techniques and controls are used to satisfy specific legal requirements, the auditor must, in his examination, consider the financial effect of noncompliance on financial statements. Therefore, in governmental auditing, there is an absolute interdependency between the financial and compliance aspects of an audit.

The relationship between financial and compliance auditing is recognized in the GAO *Standards for Audit of Governmental Organizations, Programs, Activities and Functions.* This publication expands the scope of traditional financial audits to include, as an integral part, a compliance review with applicable laws and regulations. This viewpoint differs from the AICPA's, where compliance auditing is seen as incidental to the financial audit.

The second major purpose of compliance auditing has received its impetus from the many federally funded categorical grant assistance programs. In recent years, these programs have been increasing in size, variety, and resources for program support.

With the growth in federally sponsored programs, there has been an increased effort by the federal government to improve grant administration and program effectiveness. Part of this effort has been the development of specific laws and administrative regulations to guide grant recipients in administering programs. Another facet of this effort has been the development of audit guides by most federal agencies that are designed to familiarize auditors with the basic purpose and objectives of their various programs.

Basically, the audit guides require a financial examination and a compliance review of various legal and administrative regulations. Since certain parts of the legislation authorizing the programs and subsequent administrative regulations were written to promote achievement of program objectives, it seems obvious that the compliance review is fulfilling part of the requirements for a performance review. Thus, there is an absolute interdependency between the compliance and performance aspects of an audit.

With divergent viewpoints concerning the meaning of compliance auditing, it becomes imperative that all audit engagements be explicitly written to avoid any possible misunderstandings as to what is expected from the auditor. A clear understanding by all parties concerned is especially important in this area because it has been our experience that compliance reviews for federally sponsored grants require substantial increases in audit time to meet compliance reporting requirements.

To provide the necessary independent review of the decision-making process in administering government programs, federal agencies are increasingly asking auditors to perform compliance audits. These audits, when conducted in conjunction with financial or performance audits, will significantly contribute to the current effort of improving grant administration and program effectiveness.

An extension of audit time is important to both the audit agency and the recipient of grant funds. For the audit agency, additional time means that other audit responsibilities have to be postponed or even canceled because most audit agencies always seem to have a large audit backlog. Even if audit time is made available or if outside public accountants are hired to perform the audit, the grant recipient is concerned with the problem of paying for the audit. Some federally funded programs provide for the cost of audits, but others only allow minimum audit charges or none at all.

Concepts of Compliance Auditing — Authoritative Criteria

John J. Lordan, CPA

The Internal Auditor April 1976

The auditing of government programs is more challenging today than ever before in our nation's history. Over the last several years, sharp shifts in budget priorities have resulted in management problems. In fiscal 1968, 45 percent of the federal tax dollar went to defense and 32 percent went to human resources. Today, those figures are more than reversed. The President's budget for fiscal 1976 has 27 percent going to defense and 55 percent for direct-benefit payments to individuals and grants to state and local governments. Socially oriented programs are always difficult to manage, highly fragmented, and subject to great uncertainties and frequent change. Their objectives are often unclear or conflicting, and their outputs are difficult to quantify. In many cases, even their costs are difficult to fully account for.

The mushrooming of grant programs has resulted in an extensively fragmented federal aid system. Although designed to help communities and individuals meet urgent social and economic needs, federal aid resulted in an operation in which Washington officials became the decision makers in thousands of U.S. communities.

Notwithstanding good intentions, grant programs today have great differences in size, objective, service, and funding levels. They include roads, housing, food, health services, community services, transit systems, and so on.

They are also administered in different ways: (1) by states under federal regulations; (2) funds are provided directly to the states and, in turn, are passed on to local jurisdictions; (3) and other funds go directly to local jurisdictions, organizations or individuals. In turn, these funds are often subcontracted to other organizations.

Emphasis on Audit

Even with the variety described above, some common themes run throughout. One of them is the ever-increasing demand for audits. An important element of governmental auditing is a determination as to whether an entity is complying with the requirements of applicable laws and regulations.

In 1972 the comptroller general issued *Standards for Audit of Governmental Organizations, Programs, Activities & Functions.* In 1973 the General Services Administration issued *Federal Management Circular (FMC) 73-2,* setting forth policies to be observed by executive branch agencies in the audit of federal programs.

Also, a major interagency effort resulted in the issuance of *FMC 74-7,* which establishes uniform administrative requirements for grants in aid to state and local governments and stipulated that grantee financial management systems shall provide for: "Audits to be made by the grantee or at his direction to determine, at a minimum, the fiscal integrity of financial transactions and reports, and the compliance with laws, regulations, and administrative requirements."

Compliance Criteria

Both GAO's *Standards* and *FMC* 73-2 (pp. 28-31) emphasize the importance of compliance as one of the elements of an audit program.

With regard to its standard on compliance, GAO elaborates as follows:

> "In governmental auditing, compliance with pertinent laws and regulations is particularly significant because government organizations, functions, programs, or activities are creatures of law and have more specific rules and regulations than are usually applicable to private organizations.
>
> "In making his review, the auditor . . . should select and review those laws and regulations which have a direct bearing or a significant impact upon the entity to be audited or its operations . . . As a general rule, the auditor first should find out from the audited entity's management the legal and regulatory requirements it is required to follow. He then should make his own tests to determine whether any requirements are being overlooked by the entity. Some sources of information on legal and regulatory requirements follow.

1. Legal or legislative data, including:
   a. Basic legislation
   b. Reports of hearings
   c. Legislative committee reports
   d. Annotated references from reference services covering related court decisions and legal opinions
   e. Historical data relating to the movements to achieve the legislation and similar prior legislation
   f. State constitutions, statutes, resolutions, and legislative orders
   g. Local charters, ordinances, and resolutions
2. External administrative requirements, including:
   a. Memorandums from federal, state, or local administrative agencies
   b. Guidelines and other administrative regulations affecting program operations from federal, state, or local agencies
3. Grant arrangements, when grants are involved, including:
   a. Proposals from grantees

b. Pertinent correspondence from grantors and grantees
c. Memorandums of meetings held to discuss the grants
d. The grant documents, including amendments
e. Grant regulations
f. Grant budgets and supporting schedules

* * * *

"*Financial and compliance* — The auditor is to test the financial transactions and operations of the audited organization, program, function, or activity to determine whether that entity is in compliance with pertinent laws or regulations. The auditor also is to make a review to satisfy himself that the audited entity has not incurred significant unrecorded liabilities [contingent or actual] through failure to comply with, or through violation of, pertinent laws and regulations.

"*Economy and efficiency* — The auditor is to make a review of the laws and regulations applying to any aspect . . . in which he attempts to make a judgment regarding whether existing practices can be made significantly more efficient or economical.

* * * *

Such a review is needed . . . to provide the auditor with information on constraints on the entity's authority to change its practices to make them more efficient and economical.

"*Program results* — The auditor is to review the laws and regulations pertaining to the goals and objectives of the audited entity's programs or activities in sufficient depth to gain a working understanding of the results that are expected from the programs or activities."

Audit Coordination

The policy intent of *FMC 73-2* is to promote improved audit practices, to achieve more efficient use of manpower, to improve coordination of audit efforts, and to emphasize the need for early audits of new or substantially changed programs.

Coordination of audit work, including compliance auditing, is especially important where different audit organizations have a common interest in the programs subject to audit. In this regard, *FMC 73-2* states:

> "Federal agencies will coordinate and cooperate with each other in developing and carrying out their individual audit plans. Such actions will include continuous liaison; the exchange of audit techniques, objectives, and plans; and the development of audit schedules to minimize the amount of audit effort required. Federal agencies will encourage similar coordination and cooperation among federal and non-federal audit staffs where there is a common interest in the programs subject to audit."

Use of Independent Public Accountants

For a number of years, independent public accountants have been auditing recipients of federal funds. With the advent of the expanded federal assistance programs in the 1960's, however, their involvement increased, and some problem areas have developed, notably in the area of the scope of the grant audit.

Government agencies increasingly were requiring grant audits to include review of grantee records for compliance with grant conditions. Currently, the government agencies have a pretty clear understanding of what information they must provide to independent public accountants in order to obtain the financial-compliance audit most generally employed in the grant area. Many problems, however, remain to be worked out in connection with broader-scope audits.

The Future

We can expect continuous change in the allocation of resources to meet current economic and social needs. New legislation will be enacted, and new regulations will be developed as well as frequent changes in existing laws and regulations. We can also expect the trend to continue with regard to the decentralization of responsibility from Washington to the field as well as the placing of greater reliance on the recipients of federal assistance for effective administration of such programs. All of this emphasizes the need for and importance of effective and timely audits in order to insure accountability by the executive branch to the Congress and to the public.

Auditing Financial Compliance

W. B. Bolton, CA

The Internal Auditor April 1976

Compliance is related to authority to act. In a governmental atmosphere it appears in three ways:

- Legal authority to become involved
- Budgetary authority to expend monies on matters on which you have the legal authority to become involved
- Organizational authority as evidenced by the hierarchical responsibility structure and administrative procedures which in some jurisdictions are confirmed by a procedure by law.

Legal authority is derived from public laws and may be mandatory or permissive in nature.

Mandatory legal authority requires an action by all, whereas permissive legal authority does not require an action unless the government becomes involved in the matter to which the law applies, e.g., a municipality may have authority to license a trailer park, but if there are no house trailers or if the municipality does not wish to regulate them, there is no compulsion to act.

Budgetary authority is an authority to expend monies in terms of the approved budgetary classifications . . . be they a program, objects of expenditure (salaries, materials, fixed assets), or both.

Budgetary control is related to ensuring that the monies allotted are expended for the purposes set out in the budget; for example, if the control is by program, the full amount may be expended on anything related to the program; however, if the control is by object (salaries), amounts allotted are usually not transferable, even though one category is unspent (e.g., machinery) and another is overexpended (e.g., salaries).

In this respect, there is a difference between an overexpenditure and a nonbudgeted item. The auditor should be careful to ensure that budget variances are properly identified.

Organizational authority relates to the formal administration and granting of approval "by the proper authorities." Administratively, there is both formal and informal administration. Sometimes, it is the informal administration of being able to call up "Jim" and expedite something that makes the formal administration work. However, to ensure proper allocation or assumption of responsibilities, the various approvals required in the formal administration hierarchy should be in place.

The Philosophy of Auditing Legal and Financial Compliance

It is easier to identify a problem in theory than it is to identify its occurrence in practice.

There are a few guidelines or truisms which, if followed, will enable the auditor to offer a knowledgeable opinion as to the actions of the organization which he audits:

1. The auditor must understand the aims and objectives of the organization and the legal and operational constraints within which it operates. He should also understand the peculiar requirements necessary to obtain the objectives: first, to make a realistic assessment as to whether these constraints are realistic; second that they have been complied with; and third, whether they should be changed.
2. As every action of a governmental body is taken pursuant to statutory or regulatory authority, the personal knowledge of the auditor must encompass at least the main and/or recurring "authorities."
3. An auditor's comments on compliance should be unbiased, factual, informative, and, above all, constructive rather than punitive.

The auditor should report an error in order that it may be corrected and the circumstances causing the error identified so that errors might be avoided or handled properly in the future.

Enforcement of Compliance

To be effective, the written report should be made to those who can take action to correct (or commend) those concerned.

Unless the auditor feels strong enough about a situation to recommend dismissal or discipline, his recommendations must identify the problem and offer solutions rather than merely stating that something has been done in the wrong manner.

Informal discussions between the auditor and the interested officials prior to the auditor's formulating his final report are valuable to get reactions to the problem and what went wrong with the system of internal control (which ordinarily would throw up a red flag when an action isn't appropriate).

The Use of Audit Committees

The concept of the private sector's Audit Committee, as a vehicle for discussing the implication of the auditor's recommendation and, more particularly, for ensuring that action is taken on the recommendations, could be adapted quite advantageously to governmental procedures.

If such a vehicle is set up, there should be a continuous relationship of consultation and advice rather than the adversary situation, which sometimes exists between the auditor and the management staff of the agency being audited.

Such a committee might be comprised of heads of departments and the legislative representative (minister, member of council, committee chairman, etc.) directly involved who would meet to discuss changes recommended, determine their impact on the organization, and how and when they might be implemented to improve the organization rather than punitively accusing any one.

It is sometimes not sufficiently appreciated that the auditor is as much on the "hot seat" to defend his comments as is the accountant or administrator to defend his actions. Nevertheless, if the audit is conducted on the basis of mutual trust and respect, compliance will become a guide rather than a threat to governmental officials.

Compliance Audits in San Diego County

Gerald J. Lonergan, CIA

The Internal Auditor Mar./April 1975

Auditing by its very nature is generally considered to be a dysfunctional process which accents the negative and tends to produce, more often than not, an adversary relationship between the "auditor" and "auditee." The use and connotation of the term "compliance" in connection with the audit process tends to further support the negative aspects of the audit relationship.

Webster's New Twentieth Century Dictionary defines the term compliance as "a yielding to a . . . demand, concession; submission" and provided the following example of usage:

"Let the king meet *compliance* in your looks, a free and ready yielding to his wishes. – (Rowe)"

A major thrust of our efforts in San Diego County in recent years has been to enhance the effectiveness of the auditing function through the development of better relationships with managers of operational agencies. To further emphasize the potential for utilization of audit results in the management process, we prefer to use the term "management audits." These produce management reports which are directed to managers. These reports are distinguished from the more formal and traditional financial audit reports which are issued publicly.

Reporting Procedures

In accordance with both charter and code provisions, all full-scope financial audit reports performed by the county auditor are filed concurrently with the Board of Supervisors (the governing body of the county) and the Grand Jury. All such reports become public records and are listed on the Board's official agenda. Should any formal report of audit issued by the county auditor contain any findings, recommendations, or qualification of the opinion, the officer whose operations are covered by the examination must respond in writing to both the Board of Supervisors and the Grand Jury, disclosing specific corrective actions taken or planned. Should the officer involved disagree with the findings of the county auditor or be unable to initiate corrective actions on his own, his response must explain why.

These provisions give the county auditor a powerful tool to institute or otherwise insure compliance with his recommendations. Actions by the governing body are oftentimes required (for example to make available to a county officer the resources necessary to comply). The public nature of the auditor's reports themselves, coupled with the potential for adverse criticism of the Board of Supervisors by the Grand Jury in its own reports, serves to insure that adequate attention is given to such matters.

Management Audit Report

The development of a less formalized approach was necessary to deal with financial matters of a lesser significance and to provide a vehicle for dealing with nonfinancial matters of an operational nature. Our management audit reports serve this function and provide a convenient vehicle to communicate a wide variety of informational items which are of value to operating unit managers.

All management reports are delivered personally to the officer involved by the county auditor. This provides an opportunity to discuss the matters more fully as well as to explore the potential and alternatives for indicated actions. The financial audit report is also delivered at this meeting and discussed prior to its being filed with the Board of Supervisors. Distribution of the management report is limited internally, and distribution outside of the department audited is at the discretion of the officer involved.

Our entire audit program is predicated upon the "Theory Y" behavioral science assumption that the department heads and officers being audited are honest and dedicated to discharging their assigned responsibilities as economically and efficiently as possible. Although we still must devote considerable time and effort to the conduct of audit tests of financial transactions in accordance with generally accepted auditing standards, the primary attention of our reporting is to bring items of operational significance to the attention of managers. We encourage taking full advantage of the observational skills of the 25-man field audit staff to identify potential areas for operational improvements and to transfer the knowledge gained from observing successful operations in the conduct of other examinations.

Expanding the Scope of the Audit

Initial efforts to expand the scope of audit activity into operational areas was viewed with some concern by the managers. We alleviated some of their fears by initiating a preaudit conference to discuss the audit and to request the department head to designate areas where he might like to have us examine and report exclusively to him on our findings.

Although somewhat skeptical of the assurances given with respect to limiting the disclosure of operational audit findings and recommendations to only those with the authority to implement corrective actions, our scrupulous adherence to that commitment has engendered enthusiastic support. This commitment has not, however, been applied to those infrequent occasions when fraud or other potentially criminal activities are detected. In those cases, we are obligated to disclose such information to the district attorney so that appropriate criminal prosecution action may be initiated. Since actions of this nature seldom occur within operations of the county, we entered into an arrangement with the district attorney to have an audit staff assigned on rotation to his department in order to participate in the investigation and prosecution of criminal fraud cases where the district attorney required someone knowledgeable in accounting and auditing.

In addition to providing valuable experience for the audit staff involved (which is shared with other staff members as part of our inhouse training efforts), the cooperative program has produced a record of 100% convictions on all cases where we have participated.

Specific corrective actions required to implement operational improvements are normally not recommended as it is felt that this is more properly the function of the manager who has to institute the action. Whenever appropriate, we will point out other operations where similar problems were successfully addressed and will suggest that the manager or his staff might benefit from a review of the other operations.

The Key Elements of Success

Our experience has shown that there are key elements which have materially contributed to our success in operational auditing:

- A knowledgeable, competent, and observant professional audit staff which exhibits good common sense and judgment;
- The development and maintenance of good professional-level rapport and respect between the Audit Department and operational managers through establishment of supportive policies and practices which are consistently and uniformly applied by the audit staff; and
- The ability to exercise good judgment in the determination of the approach to be used and the degree of compliance to be required with respect to recommendations which recognize the problems of operations managers, particularly with respect to making prospective judgmental decisions without the full benefit of the auditor's "hindsight."

Techniques in Compliance – Effectiveness in Auditing

Dr. Richard E. Brown and Jeffrey H. Brewer

The Internal Auditor April 1976

Outlined below are the steps taken in a compliance – effectiveness audit completed by the Kansas Legislative Division of Post Audit in December, 1975 to determine whether laws governing the use of the state's water resources were adequate to protect those resources. The audit was initiated because a series of planning studies completed in the late 1960's and early 1970's indicated that central and western Kansas, the heart of the state's rich agricultural resource, would be out of water in 45 years and that this could have a devastating effect on the state's economy and tax base.

Intent

The first objective of the audit was to identify applicable laws and their intent. Kansas law was clear. All the water in the state was dedicated to the use of its people. The State was, according to K.S.A. 82a-706, to 'control, regulate, conserve, allot, and aid in the distribution of . . .' that water. The Water Appropriation Act provided guidance on enforcement and established several specific procedures to be followed:

- To have a right to the unimpaired use of water, specific application procedures must be made to develop that right.
- To ensure that a right applied for is actually developed as approved, the law requires the applicant and the state to follow several listed procedures.
- To protect established rights from impairment, the law grants certain enforcement powers to the state and allows additional remedies through the courts.
- To ensure development and use of water rights, the law requires forfeiture of rights not developed and/or not being exercised.
- To encourage enforcement and public understanding of the law, provision was made for the establishment of rules and regulations to clarify and interpret the statute.

One important limitation in implementing the *Act* was noted. Since a permit is needed only to protect a right, water may be used without a permit. As the intent of the law was clear in calling for water-use regulation, this limitation could adversely affect its enforcement and the state's dwindling water supply.

As with most acts, even specific and detailed ones, many terms and procedures remained to be clarified and interpreted by the courts and the enforcing agency through the issuance of rules and regulations and/or policies and procedures. A search of case law, always necessary in a compliance audit, determined that the constitutionality of the law had been tested and upheld in both Kansas and federal courts. It also indicated that there was a problem as to what constituted impairment of a right.

The agency, because it had not established rules and regulations or policies and procedures on impairment, had left definition up to the courts. However, only one Kansas district court decision existed; and it did not have statewide applicability. This decision specified that impairment occurred when the yield of the well declined a minimum of 20 percent in addition to the decline caused by the well system's pump. Furthermore, Kansas courts generally relied on the state's enforcement agency as an expert witness, thus making more remote any chance of defining impairment, one of the most important sections of the *Act*. The definition established in the court case was used by the audit team as a standard for evaluating cases of potential impairment, even though its coverage was limited in that it did not have statewide applicability.

Compliance and Effectiveness

A careful reading of material on the intent of the law showed that the *Act* was passed to establish adequate administrative control over the state's water resources to prevent overdevelopment. An examination of water resources research done to date by various state and federal agencies indicated clearly that the surface and groundwater resources of western Kansas were being depleted at a rapid rate. Some areas would literally run out of water in a few years.

It was necessary to determine whether problems associated with the program were caused by the *Act* itself and the procedures resulting from it, by improper implementation of the *Act*, or by a combination of both. The auditors carefully examined the enforcement agency's records and procedures in order to determine the best methods for measuring the various processes described in the intent section and their effectiveness in protecting individual water rights and conserving the state's water resources.

A statistically valid sample of applications for appropriate water was drawn in attempt to determine whether the procedures required by law were being followed. An evaluation of the sample showed that, while many of the mechanical procedures described in the law were being followed, key elements in the process were not (e.g., protecting existing water users from impairment and preventing overdevelopment). As a result, virtually everyone who applied for a permit received one. The agency allowed this to occur because, while under the law, water could be used without a permit, once a permit was granted, the agency had a measure of control over a water user. This approach, of course, aggravated problems associated with both potential impairment and overdevelopment.

Another audit procedure was developed to partially measure the extent of water use without a permit by testing procedures relating to a new state law administered by another state agency. This law requires well drillers to be licensed and to report all wells drilled to the state. A sample of wells reported showed that 60 percent of the wells drilled were not covered by an application to use water and that another 23 percent were drilled before the application was approved. Thus, no matter how effectively the Water Appropriation Act is enforced, most persons are not getting permits before drilling — a clear violation of the intent (that water use be controlled) but not of the letter of the law.

Two recommendations were made in the audit report covering these issues. Corrective legislation was proposed to require all persons wishing to use water to get a permit prior to doing so. It was also recommended that the enforcing agency clarify, interpret, and enforce all sections of the law.

The sample of applications was also used to judge the agency's program to ensure that water rights were established within a reasonable time and that, once established, they were recognized by the state so that they were protected. Again, the law cited specific steps to be taken which were measurable through the sample. The auditors found that the state was not effectively performing any of the tasks required by law in monitoring the development of water rights and, therefore, recommended appropriate measures .

It was more difficult to evaluate the protection of established water rights from impairment as there were no established standards for defining impairment. A procedure for processing complaints did exist, and this was examined. A sample of complaints showed that the formal procedure was rarely followed. It also showed that, where impairment had been found, the agency never used its formally established procedure to terminate the impairment. Also, the lack of written information on why impairment was found in specific cases made it difficult to determine the bases for the decisions.

Finally, a statistically valid sample of persons with established water rights was taken to determine whether these persons continued to maintain their water rights as determined through a reporting procedure required by the agency. The sample showed that, although 18 percent of all water users had apparently abandoned their water rights, less than one percent had been terminated according to procedures established by law. The auditors again recommended that the procedures established by law be followed.

Conclusion

The compliance-effectiveness audit demonstrated that the agency was not effective in complying with or enforcing major sections of the *Act.* It also showed the law to be defective in certain key areas. Moreover, the audit clearly documented the extent of developing water shortages in central and western Kansas. While the audit did not link the lack of compliance directly to the water shortage, the potential linkage was made evident. The Kansas Legislature was given several proposals for legislative change, and the agency was given recommendations to improve its compliance with the law. At the time of this writing, these proposals are being reviewed and discussed by the 1976 Legislature.

Atomic Energy Commission Performs Agency-Wide Management Audits

Richard J. Griffin, Jr., CPA

The Internal Auditor July/Aug. 1973

The Atomic Energy Commission (AEC) is an independent agency of the federal government. The Commission is responsible to the President and the Congress, and consists of five members – one of which is the chairman. The administrative and executive efforts related to encouraging the use of atomic energy are directed by the general manager, who reports to the commission. The control aspects of atomic energy activites are directed by the director of regulation, who reports to the commission.

AEC operations cost about $2.6 billion per year, with management direction for carrying out specific programs being decentralized in 10 field offices located through the United States. Industrial firms and educational or other nonprofit organizations perform, in Government-owned facilities, most of the work involved in achieving AEC goals. These firms operate under cost reimbursement contracts administered primarily by the managers of the 10 field offices.

Policy Requires Internal Auditing

It is the policy of AEC that internal auditing be an element in the administration of operations performed by AEC and its cost-type contractors. Internal auditing – in addition to ascertaining the allowability of expenditures, realization of revenues and compliance with AEC directives and contract provisions – includes reviews of the business practices and procedures which have an impact upon the financial interests of AEC. Some areas specifically identified in the AEC Audit Handbook for audit coverage are:

- budget execution and fiscal accounting
- contracting and procurement
- receiving and inspection
- warehousing and inventory control
- management of capital assets
- surplus property
- motor pool operations
- traffic
- administrative services
- personnel and payroll practices and controls
- travel practices and controls
- insurance
- cash controls
- cost distribution and product cost accounting
- financial accounting and reporting

However, the auditors are not limited to any particular areas and may inquire into any matters they consider appropriate.

In AEC, the controller – who reports to the commission and the general manager – is responsible for establishing agency audit policy, for performing audits of direct government activities at AEC Headquarters and at the 10 AEC field offices, and for the technical adequacy of audits of contract activities. The assistant controller for auditing has been designated by the controller to carry out these responsibilities. The managers of the field offices, under the AEC audit policy, are responsible for carrying out the audits of contract activities. These include the 40 contractors operating AEC-owned facilities such as the national laboratories performing research, gaseous diffusion plants producing enriched uranium and sites for testing reactor and weapon components.

AEC-Wide Audits

One particularly effective audit technique is the performance of concurrent audits of a particular subject at all AEC field offices and the AEC-owned contractor-operated facilities. The application of this technique in AEC is referred to as "AEC-Wide Audits."

The results of the reviews are included in individual audit reports issued to the manager of each office or contract facility covered. A consolidated report is also prepared and includes the more significant findings developed at each office and contractor location, and reported in the individual reports, as well as overall audit conclusions and appropriate recommendations for management action. The consolidated report is addressed to the General Manager and to the five Commissioners. It is transmitted to each field office manager and contractor with a request for a reply within a stated period identifying actions taken on report recommendations. In addition to achieving corrective action or management improvements at the operating level, the report serves as a basis for initiating, implementing, changing or clarifying overall agency policies.

During the 10-year period since initiation of AEC-wide audits, a broad range of subjects has been covered including:

- negotiated fixed-price procurements
- advance financing of operating-contractor operations
- travel to foreign countries and attendance at foreign meetings
- motor vehicle activities
- outside training
- management action on audit findings and recommendations
- transportation of property
- post-award review of certified cost or pricing data used in negotiating fixed-price procurements
- employment and compensation of consultants
- stores inventory activities
- employee relocation costs
- equipment management activities
- controls over computer resources.

Normally, two AEC-wide audits are scheduled each year. The subjects are selected and the audit programs are prepared by the Controller's audit staff. Considerable assistance is provided by field office auditors. Such assistance includes the review of each proposed audit program for the purpose of offering constructive comments and suggestions and help in making pilot tests at one or more locations. The audits are performed at AEC field offices by the Controller's audit staff and at AEC contractor-operated facilities by field office audit staffs.

Selectively, the audits performed by the field office audit staffs are reviewed by members of the Controller's audit staff prior to release of the final audit report. This is to assure that the audit is carried out consistent with the audit program and that the resulting audit report is prepared in a manner that will facilitate preparation of the consolidated AEC-wide report.

Results

This audit technique provides the commission and the general manager with a profile on the management or operation of a particular subject throughout the AEC. The consolidated report includes a comparison of selected operating data or audit results for each office and contractor. A positive effort is made to present the favorable and unfavorable findings in a balanced manner as well as to point up those offices and contractors where management attention is required.

With the diversity of operations and the many offices and contractors involved, considerable effort is required to program, coordinate and direct the performance of the AEC-wide audits.

However, the AEC-wide audits have been most favorably received by AEC management and the results have more than justified the efforts.

Economy and Efficiency Audits In Local Government

Lloyd F. Hara

The Internal Auditor Mar./April 1975

Is your organization operating efficiently and economically?

Since government does not have a profit and loss statement, the economy and efficiency audit has been used to evaluate our economy and efficiency of operations. The General Accounting Office's standards for government auditing defines the economy and efficiency audit to determine "whether the entity is managing or utilizing its resources (personnel, property, space, and so forth) in an economical and efficient manner and the causes of any inefficiencies and uneconomical practices, including any inadequacies in management information systems, administrative procedures, or organizational structures." It is within this context that we will discuss some aspects of economy and efficiency audits.

Traditionally, the fiscal-legal compliance audit meets most local government requirements. Correspondingly, the local auditor offices only possess limited audit skill levels and budgets. Today, the economy and efficiency audit and program effectiveness audit are being emphasized.

Awareness: Key Ingredient

A key ingredient for a successful economy and efficiency audit is being aware of the audit environment. One factor is timing: When do you conduct an audit? Events beyond the control of the auditor oftentimes provide an opportunity to effectively perform an audit. A case in point is the recent energy crisis, which opened the door to examine motor pool operations and utilization of vehicles, especially those of elected and key appointed officials. The report may be received with no opposition, and recommendations could be implemented as displaying public concern toward energy conservation and economy.

Depending on the audit objectives, time, and resources available, the auditor assigns priority to his mandatory and statutory requirements but usually has an opportunity to examine economy and efficiency areas. Special emphasis should be given to areas which have received wide public attention or which have the greatest dollar impact. In most cases, it is apparent where productivity and cost savings may be implemented.

One begins to raise questions such as: How does one perform this activity? What is accomplished? What is expected to be accomplished (goals or targets)? What has been done to improve service and costs? What problems are encountered, etc.?

Answers to questions like these and personal observation of the work process will cause one to focus on areas for more in-depth data collection and analysis.

What to Look For

General observation may detect conditions such as:

Manpower

Excessive idle, nonproductive, sick, and accidental time loss; excessive turnover; and unbalanced work loads

Equipment

Excessive repairs, unused capacity, lack of equipment and supplies, outdated equipment, and large inventory and supplies

Space

Unused floor spaces, overcrowding, distribution and poor work flow, archaic storage practices, and level of building maintenance and repair

Utility & Miscellaneous

Delays in printing, communication costs, insurance coverage (duplicating coverages), overheating and lighting (energy conservation)

These examples will lead one to examine closely whether the expense to maintain existing practices are cost-justified. The auditor assigned should possess expertise and experience to adequately perform and to build credibility in conducting the economy audit. The establishment of performance criteria is another critical factor. This may be accomplished in several ways: (1) The easiest manner is to utilize an existing standards manual from a recognized source or (2) to establish a comparative standard within one's own organization based on an internal history of performance.

Work Standards

There are many comparable work activities in private industry where work standards have been established. For example, skills requiring repetitive activity have been historically documented and tested, like clerical skills: typing, filing, mail room activity, etc. Other areas such as trades also have estimated time values for conducting certain types of jobs such as electrical, mechanical, and plumbing. Standard rate books have been established to determine cost/job activity. Wherever certain nationally accepted standards have been established, the auditor can confidently use the standard as a basis for evaluation.

The development of one's own standards for comparison is also useful, especially where an activity is unique or no standards are available. Standard work measurement techniques may be used to measure output and establish a baseline of activity for future evaluation. Then one performs a second work measurement to determine whether or not the activity is more cost effective or economical. The auditor-developed standards have more meaning if the auditee also plays a key role in their development. Once standards have been jointly agreed to, the acceptance of auditor findings is improved.

Improving Costs Effectively

The auditor must constantly search for methods to improve costs versus services within the total context of an activity. One must be careful that reducing certain costs does not increase other costs or greatly reduce services. This brings to mind a case where a city light crew had a backup truck . . . usually in storage. The truck was eliminated as a cost-saving measure, but this proved to be very expensive in lost productive time because light crews were idle when their only truck was disabled.

Can you conclude that your organization is operated efficiently and economically, or can you spot additional areas for improvement?

Auditing for Efficiency and Economy

Martin Ives, CIA, CPA

The Internal Auditor Jan./Feb. 1975

Spiraling inflation and deepening recession are placing an increasing burden on the revenue-expenditure structures of state and local governments. With less real dollars available to accomplish their programs, the efficiency with which government managers spend their resources will have a major impact on the effectiveness of their programs. Auditing for efficiency and economy thus takes on increasing significance in the current economic climate.

An analysis of the New York State comptroller's audit reports on state and city agencies shows that the findings related to efficiency and economy tend to fall into the following categories:

Inadequate Personnel Utilization

Inadequate personnel utilization is caused by such factors as weak supervision and lack of performance standards, results in insufficient productivity, lack of attention to duty, and failure to assign personnel to duties where they could be most productive.

Item: The city's public assistance case load contained an intolerable degree of ineligible persons. A quality control system designed to measure the level of ineligibility and to highlight procedural weaknesses contributing to the problem was experiencing inordinate delays. Our audit showed that a major cause of this delay was poor supervision and absence of work standards for the quality control employees. Thus, the failure to efficiently implement a key managerial control was contributing to the continued waste of program funds.

Item: Audit of the Tax Department showed that, despite increasing backlogs of work, vacant tax auditor positions were not being filled and many of the filled positions were "on loan" to less productive units. We concluded that the department was being "penny wise and pound foolish," since every dollar spent on tax enforcement produced many additional dollars of tax revenue and since the potential for collecting delinquent taxes tended to decrease with the passage of time.

Item: An audit at the junior high schools showed that many teachers had an unusually large number of "administrative hours," performing nonteaching clerical tasks. There was a potential either for using the teachers by reducing class sizes, presumably increasing the effectiveness of the teaching program, or by replacing a portion of the teaching staff with lower-paid clerical personnel.

Item: Audit of employee attendance and activities at various unannounced times during the day, evening, night, and weekend shifts disclosed many instances of employees sleeping on the job, congregating in offices, arriving late for work, and leaving early. This condition was a major factor in the poor level of patient care at a state hospital.

Basic Managerial Weaknesses

Basic managerial weaknesses are manifested in inadequate planning, lack of effective management reporting systems, and failure to seek out and follow up on the implications of available comparative cost data.

Item: Our comparative analysis of state and private schools for the treatment of youthful offenders showed significant variations in the portions of their budgets spent for education, treatment, and administration. Private schools were spending far more funds on program activities such as education and psychiatric services, while the state schools were spending more on administrative costs. Agency management should have obtained such comparative data and evaluated their implications.

Item: Drug addicts were treated at numerous facilities throughout the state. Our audit showed that per diem costs ranged from $23 to $47. There was a need for management to evaluate the program implications of this wide disparity in costs among the various facilities so as to maximize program accomplishment and minimize the costs.

Consolidation of Activities and "Make-or-Buy" Analyses

Major cost reductions are possible through consolidation of activities and "make-or-buy" analyses. This potential exists with regard to both support functions and program activities.

Item: A separate hospital with its own administrative staff occupied three buildings on the grounds of another state hospital. Our audit showed that the limited work load of the administrative activities of this separate hospital and its proximity to the offices of the main hospital would permit consolidation of the administrative functions of the two hospitals at a savings of $145,000 a year.

Item: A local school district exercised control over 29 individual facilities. Our audit showed that the unutilized classroom facilities amounted to about 28 percent or the equivalent of eight schools and that enrollment was continuing to decline. We recommended consolidating and closing of individual facilities to the extent feasible. Such action would not only reduce costs but also provide greater flexibility in class sizes and course offerings.

Inadequate Management of Assets

Inadequate management of assets resulted in the loss of funds and/or the needless tie-up of funds.

Item: The outstanding accounts receivable at a teaching hospital increased from $7 million to $11 million during a two-year period. An audit showed that this serious situation was caused in part by a lack of aggressive follow-up action, insufficient supervision, and insufficient staff to keep up with an increasing work load.

Item: More than $6 million in available federal funds were being lost each year because of the failure to bill certain outpatient services. An audit showed that the problem was caused by the inability of the state and local officials to agree upon a billing format.

The foregoing illustrations suggest that improved productivity in government and more effective delivery of government services will be brought about through innovative management, close supervision, and comparative analysis of costs and methods. There is ample opportunity for the auditor to play a key role in this process.

Effectiveness Evaluations

John W. Fawsett, CIA

The Internal Auditor Jan./Feb. 1974

In the May/June 1973 issue of *The Internal Auditor* I wrote on a technique – Performance Analysis and Planning – that we find quite useful in Army Audit Agency management audits. In this article, I'm going to explore something more basic – the evaluation of effectiveness. Unless this part of the management audit is approached and executed correctly, it is highly doubtful that the main purpose of the management audit – improved performance in the major mission areas – will be attained.

What Level of Performance Is Acceptable?

Perhaps one of the worst mistakes an auditor can make is to cause an improvement in one area at the expense of another more important area. But this could happen unless the auditor makes a concerted effort to determine the relative priorities of the various missions and activities included in the audit.

In the current environment of extreme economy (current, at least, in the Army), management does not have the capability or resources to do all things equally well. Thus, priorities are established, resources are allocated, and sometimes even relatively poor performance becomes acceptable in less important areas. The good auditor recognizes this "poor performance" as the price paid to do more important things better and looks for improvements possible *within the resources available to this area.* The poor auditor pushes the panic button recommending major changes in controls, procedures, and allocation of resources – all of which, if management decides not to resist, will only serve to cause a decrease in performance in more important areas. Of course, if management has *not* established priorities when resources are limited, this should be a major audit area leading to development of a selective management and resource allocation program geared toward insuring that the most important things are done well.

Is Performance Effective?

One of the best methods of evaluating effectiveness is to look at the results. A review of the internal operating reports is a good starting point. But don't make the mistake of relying upon these reports until their reasonableness has been verified! Too many operating reports show good performance when performance is bad.

Simultaneously, review the degree of user satisfaction. If you are auditing a supply activity, customers who aren't receiving equipment, parts, or supplies when they need them, are quick to let you know their views. Similarly, employers in a city or state can provide valuable information concerning the effectiveness of a program for training the unskilled. Of course, the auditor has to put this information in perspective and cannot make a determination that there was poor performance based upon just a few isolated instances.

Here are the basic questions the auditor should answer:

- Are good results being achieved?
- Are better results desired?
- How can improvements be made within the resources available?

"Selling" the Audit Results

The determination that improvements are needed *and feasible* is the basic determination around which the entire audit centers. Unless this determination is valid, *and is accepted as valid by management,* either recommendations will be made that won't really improve things or – and perhaps this is worse – management will reject good recommendations because they don't believe a significant problem exists. Thus, as part of the audit the auditor should determine what management reports are relied upon by activity heads to evaluate the effectiveness of operations. Inconsistencies between these reports and the audit conclusions must be reconciled and discussed with the activity head to insure that he agrees with the validity of the audit conclusions.

Often problems are known but the activity head believes he is already doing all he can to solve them. The auditor must avoid theoretically perfect solutions that require unattainable capability to implement in favor of practical, workable recommendations that can be implemented within the resources available to the auditee. The goal should be to cause a significant improvement – not to attain perfection. Further, the recommendations should be discussed sufficiently to insure that the activity head is actually convinced that the recommendations are workable and that a significant improvement will result.

Program Evaluation and the Government Internal Auditor

Dr. C. David Baron, CPA

The Internal Auditor Mar./April 1974

Although the root ideas are much older indeed, developments in internal auditing over the past decade have resulted in the general acceptance of a concept of auditing – known by various terms – that encompasses a concern for the efficiency and effectiveness of operations.

Many feel that the greatest potential for this type of auditing lies in its application to governmental organizations, indeed, a great deal of the work in developing audit systems of this nature has been pioneered by government auditors.

In this regard, I wish to focus on a particular aspect of these broad-scope audits, namely, the government auditor's concern with the benefits or accomplishments of a particular program or operation under review.

The literature in governmental auditing generally subscribes to the notion that the internal auditor should be concerned with the results and performance of government programs. However, there has been a reluctance to assign any direct responsibility to the auditor for program evaluation per se.

By and large, spokesmen have retained the internal auditor in his customary role as a compliance-investigator; reviewing a program performance report previously prepared by management so as to determine if the report is in substantial agreement with certain standards for measuring and reporting such data.

Recently-published government audit standards take this position[1], although not, apparently, in as strong terms as those used by a frequent contributor to the literature in governmental accounting and auditing. Here is his statement:

> It is not the responsibility of the auditor to find out what happened and report it, rather it is management's responsibility. The auditor examines and evaluates the information reported by management and thereby adds reliability to the report by his expression of an opinion or judgment on its fairness[2].

This is a familiar concept of auditing, perhaps useful in rationalizing the attest function of the external financial auditor, but unnecessarily constraining when applied to the emerging role of the government internal auditor.

The major flaw in this idea is that it doesn't sufficiently consider the vast potential inherent in the government internal audit function to act directly as an initiating agent in bringing about organizational improvement. The great opportunities for government internal auditors lay not so much in compliance auditing, in whatever form that might assume, but in direct involvement in the measurement and reporting of program performance and productivity.

Reflection on the unique nature of government auditing will serve to justify this point of view.

It is well known that for a commercial enterprise, the accomplishments of a particular operation or venture can be expressed in terms of profit contribution, whereas the results of a government program are much less amenable to measurement. Because of this, the manager of a commercial enterprise can rely on a formalized continuous data collection system that will provide him with a more or less constant flow of profitability reports to be used in performance evaluation.

To the government manager however, the continuous collection

[1]U.S. General Accounting Office, *Standards for Audit of Governmental Organizations, Programs, Activities, and Functions,* 1972, p. 9.

[2]Lennis M. Knighton, "Performance Auditing In Better Perspective," *The Internal Auditor,* March/April, 1973, p. 42.

of performance statistics is a much less attractive alternative for a number of reasons. Among these is the difficulty of settling on a single standard measure of performance. To an extent greater than his corporate counterpart, a government manager must rely on special studies – audits if you will – that will supply him with essential evaluative information on the status of ongoing programs.

For this reason, the government internal audit has a potential for becoming an integral part of the periodic management review and improvement cycle in the planning and control of government programs.

Viewed from this perspective, there are sound reasons for arguing that the government internal auditor should incorporate into his scope-of-audit the development of program performance standards in cooperation with operating personnel, and the subsequent measurement of program performance should become a part of his regular audit.

To be sure, the difficulties that will be faced by government audit staffs in performing this function will be great.

However, a continued emphasis on the compliance approach can be expected to produce diminishing returns as the overall quality of government management improves.

On the other hand, a program evaluation component in the periodic audit can be expected to prove rewarding not only in terms of personal satisfaction, but also in terms of an enlarged purchase on status for the auditor.

One of the priority questions confronting government managers is: "What are the results?" The internal auditor's performance or direction of special studies designed to provide answers to this question can be expected to produce a significant increase in his influence within the organization.

Auditing for the Effectiveness of Program Results in Local Governments

Dr. Meyer Drucker, CPA

The Internal Auditor Mar./April 1975

Auditing for the effectiveness of program results is new, even in operational auditing, but highly important, since it focuses on whether management controls have been established to fulfill the goals for which the department or agency was created. This type of review gets at the heart of whether the activity is accomplishing its intended mission.

Internal auditing can play a very important role provided the auditor has broad vision and the internal auditing function is independent of the program being reviewed. In fact, an internal auditing department, properly functioning, should pinpoint areas for improving revenues and cutting costs. In today's economic environment, this is vital for the survival of some government activities.

Relationship of Management and the Internal Auditor

Management often needs to be convinced of the value of operational auditing because there is the continuous cost of staffing. Its value may not always be so visible to the general public. However, an effective auditing department can and should be the eyes and ears of management.

In a few instances, the performance standards may be explicit from legislative intent. At the other extreme, the objectives for the activity may not be clearly established. Then the auditor must identify performance criteria on the basis of similar projects in other governments and then recommend actions so that the objectives will be brought into sharper focus.

Of course, it is up to the local legislative body to require better means of measuring performance. The auditor simply cannot operate in a vacuum as he serves at the pleasure of management. The philosophy of managing any governmental unit, function, or activity is set by top management: the legislative body and the chief administrative officials. However, the auditor must understand that, in operational auditing, management cannot and should not make everything explicit. It is up to the auditor to be creative and make independent evaluations to insure economical, efficient, and effective performance.

Examples of Program Results

Any program or activity which requests scarce funds from the citizenry it serves should have goals and objectives to accomplish. In local governments, this can be very tangible: the building of a highway or curbs and gutters. In many instances, the end product might be more intangible such as measuring the benefits from adding more policemen.

Standards of performance need to be determined so that the expenditures can be evaluated and controlled. Did the paving of the highway accomplish the objective of moving traffic to suburbia? Were other foreseen problems created? The areas along the highway might have been made less desirable for residential living. More slums might have been created, causing more social costs in the long run and also a cut in the potential tax base. If more law enforcement officials are hired, what kind should they be? Will the "tough man" in the street respond to new methods involving psychology and other human relations techniques or to the more forceful but "traditional cop"?

It will be difficult to establish standards in these areas, but the public should have some notion of whether the expenditures are wisely made and beneficial. This same type of analysis can be applied in virtually all local governmental activities.

Where the Auditor Should Concentrate His Efforts

The traditional financial audit has limited utility for local governments.

It is the review of operations that can assist management to do a better job. Therefore, the auditor should concentrate much of his efforts in the area of evaluating program results.

Auditing for Effectiveness

Dr. Lennis M. Knighton

The Internal Auditor Jan./Feb. 1975

One of the most exciting developments in state auditing in recent years has been the introduction of what most state authorities today refer to as "the program audit." This term refers to those aspects of an audit effort which are designed to evaluate the effectiveness of program results.

The purpose of this brief article is to outline a few of the important issues and considerations relevant to the evaluation of program results and to point out the potential benefits for such audits for improving the quality of public programs.

THE OBJECTIVES OF A PROGRAM AUDIT

Three basic questions provide the keys to effective program evaluation. First, what was accomplished? Second, was the program successful? Third, is there an adequate and appropriate control system to insure future success? Let's look at these three questions more closely.

What Was Accomplished?

In the public sector, accomplishment is not measured by the generation of revenues except in a few special cases. Rather, performance evaluators must look to one of three measures or indicators: outputs, benefits, or impacts.

"Outputs" refers to the services rendered, the goods produced, or the assistance given through public programs. Measures like students taught, cases processed, investigations made, reports completed, and examinations made are all examples of outputs. Such measures indicate work loads handled and give an important indication of the size of work force required and supporting services and other such requirements. Outputs are often difficult to measure for public-sector programs, but they are an essential part of program evaluation.

"Benefits" refers to the effect of outputs on those for whom programs are carried out. In other words, it is the benefit received by the target group that comprises the second type of measure or indicator of accomplishment. For example, the number of students taught in an educational program is an output; but the increased knowledge, skill, motivation, and aspiration levels of students are examples of benefits derived from the educational programs by the students, who are the target group in this case. Benefits are more difficult to measure than outputs, but they are more relevant to the evaluation of program accomplishment where they can be measured.

"Impacts" refers to the effect of program outputs and benefits on the community, on society as a whole, or on the world in general. Admittedly, these impacts are extremely difficult to determine; but they do comprise an additional type of measure or indicator of accomplishment if they can be obtained.

The program auditor must be conscious of the differences in these three types of measures or indicators as he seeks information on which to make judgments about program results. However, it is likely that most of his evaluation of accomplishment will center on outputs and benefits.

Was The Program Successful?

A program is successful if the objectives for which it was designed are accomplished. Effectiveness is a term that refers to "how successful we have been in accomplishing our objectives." Thus, to evaluate the success or effectiveness of programs, we must first identify the objectives being pursued through the program. We must also identify the criteria and standards by which a judgment about effectiveness can be made. Performance criteria are those statistics or items of information that have been selected from all possible indicators of performance as being especially relevant to performance evaluation and, therefore, the basis upon which judgment is to be made. Performance standards are the qualitative statements which serve as reference points or bench marks against which actual performance may be judged. For example, reading speed may be selected as a criterion for evaluating the effectiveness of a bilingual education program. Others should also be selected so that judgment is not based solely on one criterion. Using reading speed as an example, one still cannot conclude that a student's reading is good or poor until he has a standard. If students are expected to achieve a reading speed of 250 words per minute, we will judge each student's performance by this standard. So it is with all programs. We must know the objectives *and* the criteria and standards if we are to judge the success or effectiveness of programs.

What of the Control System?

Good performance is a product of good management in most cases, and good management requires an effective and appropriate control system to insure that programs are carried out as intended. Much could be said about the elements of control, the types of control systems, and the relationship of control to planning and performance evaluation; but space does not permit it here. It is imperative, however, that we underscore the fact that the program auditor has not performed his most useful function if he only evaluates the effectiveness of past programs and fails to evaluate the control system to determine that it is adequate and appropriate to insure future success.

THE BASIS OF EVALUATION

As with any other aspect of audit effort, the evaluation of the effectiveness of program results must be based upon sound evidence. This is one of the most basic standards of auditing. It is particularly important in an area where the auditor may easily be accused of being biased, politically motivated, incompetent, or unqualified. The evidence must be obtained and evaluated carefully by competent methods. The conclusions must flow from the evidence. The auditor must never allow his *a priori* judgments to dictate his search for evidence in order to marshall support for such conclusions.

Evidence to support program evaluations may be obtained from several sources. Some of it is collected systematically through the accounting system and other information channels. Other information is available through analysis, through statistical sampling, and through survey research.

Final judgments concerning effectiveness require a comparison of actual accomplishment with objectives as set forth in plans. Where objectives and standards, as explained above, are available to the evaluator, he has little difficulty in organizing his evidence of actual accomplishment in a way that will facilitate judgment. Where such objectives and standards are not clearly set forth, as is the case for most public-sector programs today, the auditor must use his professional judgment in organizing and setting forth the evidence of his examination in such a way as to permit the users of his report to make their own judgments about effectiveness. This does not preclude the auditor from offering his own opinions, observations, or conclusions; but he must be extra careful to provide for the independent judgment of others based upon the evidence collected.

THE POTENTIAL BENEFITS OF PROGRAM AUDITS

In an era when government expenditures are multiplying manyfold, it is imperative that public officials use every available tool to promote effectiveness in public programs so that the vast resources committed to such programs are not wasted. We must find out where we are accomplishing our objectives effectively and where we are falling short. Many programs have been designed to assist in this effort, including new approaches to budgeting, improved management methods, the development of more extensive reporting systems, and the extension of audit programs. In the judgment of this author, no other approach holds greater promise for achieving this goal than does program auditing. By whatever name it is called – operational auditing, performance auditing, effectiveness auditing, results auditing, or program auditing – this development in state government promises to become one of the most dominating influences in public administration in the years ahead.

Measuring Employee Perceptions And Management Auditing

Guy K. Zimmerman

The Internal Auditor May/June 1974

The U.S. Department of Labor's Office of Internal Audit has developed and is utilizing a system to measure employee perceptions of Departmental operations. The Management Audit Survey (MAS) was described by Edward J. McVeigh, former Associate Assistant Secretary for Program Review and Audit as:

> ". . . a system for analyzing employee perceptions of organizational operations. Its purpose is to aid supervisors and managers in making better use of the Department's resources to promote greater worker satisfaction and to enable the Department to do its work more effectively."

Questionnaire to Assess Human Resource Management

The survey consists of a 100 item questionnaire designed to assess nineteen areas of human resource management.[1] The questionnaire is administered to all Departmental employees and a score is obtained for each work group in which five or more employees respond. Work units with less than five or more respondents are combined with the next higher level work unit. Each score area is measured by four to six questions. Each question used in a score area has shown a high statistical relationship with the other questions used to measure that score.

The scoring results are presented in two different formats. The first format, the percentile rank, shows how well the organization did in relation to the average of all employees in the Agency or Department who completed the survey. The second format shows in absolute terms the percentage of favorable responses.

Many Factors Affect Interpretation

The survey results of course, must be interpreted in light of a number of factors such as management's interest and support of the program, changes in the organization or program structure, budgetary factors, rumors concerning the program or organization, the amount of control different levels of management may or may not have over the program, and the number of employees responding to the questionnaire. In any case, the system accords the manager the opportunity to evaluate his unit against the Agency or Department and/or in absolute terms against itself, after which, he can take whatever corrective action

[1]The nineteen areas are: Fairness of Management, Delegation of Authority, Supervisory Effectiveness, Planning and Administrative Efficiency, Climate for Innovation, Work Satisfaction, Training Effectiveness, Performance Feedback, Equal Opportunity for Women, Equal Opportunity for Minorities, Opportunity for Promotions, Downward Communication, Upward Communication, Satisfaction with Pay, Morale, Physical Working Conditions and Equipment, Co-Worker Cooperation, Operational Efficiency, and Workload Balance.

he deems necessary. The auditors and the manager have an opportunity to measure the effectiveness of any corrective actions which have been taken when the questionnaire is administered again in the future.

Audit Use of MAS

The MAS was developed, tested and utilized almost totally independently of the operational audit function. However, there have been experiments using the survey results in several audits. In one case, an audit was conducted of an organization in which the questionnaire had previously been administered. The auditors did not examine the results of the MAS until after the audit had been completed. Interestingly, the audit findings and the results of the MAS were in agreement.

In a second case, the auditors reviewed the results of the MAS as a kind of preliminary survey prior to conducting the on-site work. In that instance, the MAS was helpful because it pinpointed possible problem areas for the auditors thus saving them time.

On a third occasion, the MAS was conducted concurrently with the audit and was considered an integral part of the audit. In this case, not only was the MAS conducted but follow-up interviews were made in an attempt to identify some of the causes of the problems identified by the employees.

Of the three approaches, the third seems to be the most effective from the audit standpoint. The first allows the auditor to either confirm or refute his findings. The second approach saves time but may also bias some of the findings. The third method not only allows the auditor time to review and utilize the findings of the MAS, but it also allows time for indepth probing for causes which in turn may yield possible solutions to problem areas.

Future Use of MAS

Future use of the MAS in conjunction with operational audits provides some obvious advantages. First and foremost, it provides an input by all employees into the audit process. This is particularly important in a large organization where it is impossible for auditors to interview all employees. It also gives information to the auditor on how employees perceive their organization. This may have a greater impact on organizational operations than how the auditors and management perceive the organization. In addition, it will assist in scheduling which organizations should be audited first. Lastly, it gives the auditor a better and fuller view of the organization and assists him in identifying problem areas and determining the validity of his findings.

MAS Shows Real Potential

The Management Audit Survey to date has shown real potential as a methodology for analyzing organizations. While its utilization in conjunction with audits in the Department of Labor has been minimal in the past, its use and impact on future audits will increase thus improving the quality of the audit findings.

6
staffing

Expanding the scope of the audit function has had a profound effect on the audit staff. In the past, auditors needed to be accountants in order to perform audits. But today accounting expertise is required primarily for the financial segment of the full-scope audit. Audit staffs expected to be active in compliance, management (efficiency), and effectiveness aspects must be made up of experts in many disciplines. Generally, auditors are essentially experts in management control and do not require a knowledge of substantive areas being audited. However, government audits are facilitated if the staff is composed of economists, political scientists, statisticians, social scientists, psychologists, public administrators, management specialists, and industrial engineers.

Auditors must have the expertise to conduct audits for which they are responsible. If this expertise is not available on the staff, it must be obtained from other staffs or by engaging consultants.

Experience and capability are universal requirements in auditing, and the audit process is similar for all segments of full-scope auditing. Regardless of their specialized backgrounds, auditors must master the basics of the audit function. There should also be a provision for continuing education in auditing through professional development programs.

A knowledge of managerial concepts is very important to the operational audit staff. Because auditors evaluate management systems, they must be aware of management concepts, components, and methods of operation. Correspondingly, they must be well versed in behavioral concepts of the audit operation so they can use the participative approach to auditing now beginning to emerge. Human relations properly practiced can turn an adverse relationship into a cooperative venture.

Independence is an important consideration of staff performance. Auditors who are not objective and free from constraints are ineffective. The environment in which the audit is conducted must be free of impairment or pressures that prevent auditors from providing impartial and considered opinions and conclusions, and from reporting factual information as they see it. Personal constraints, constraints imposed by others, and constraints resulting from the organizational placement of the audit activity tend to affect or destroy independence. Auditors must be alert to note evidence of any such constraints.

Training in areas where required competence is lacking should be available to the staff. Training should also keep the staff abreast of current operational developments and the latest audit techniques. Good interpersonal attitudes are probably among the most effective means of achieving cooperation and good reception by auditees and clients. The right attitudes can be developed in the staff through progressive and innovative training sessions.

Many staffs are not large enough to provide specialists in all disciplines essential for conducting audits in all functions of the government organization. A staff may lack expertise in specialized areas such as computer operations, statistics, or operations research. It may lack specialists in substantive areas such as personnel management, procurement, loan activities, or security. Or it may lack expertise in support disciplines such as psychology, sociology, economics, or engineering. When such conditions arise, auditors may be required to engage consultants from peer audit groups, colleges and universities, management, specialized consulting firms, and even from the auditee organization itself. Capability in these areas is essential for well-conducted audits and, in many cases, to lend credibility to audit results.

Auditors should motivate their staffs to perform efficiently and effectively. Good internal communication, rewards for top performance, corrective activity couched in an environment of candor, and cooperation and loyalty outwardly displayed are some techniques that will help develop and maintain an aggressive, interested, imaginative, and innovative audit staff.

The articles in this chapter discuss in considerable detail many of the subjects briefly mentioned above. Auditor independence is discussed in two articles. E. William Rine, deputy inspector general of the Law Enforcement Assistance Administration of the U.S. Department of Justice, writes of the personal impairments aspect, whereas Jack Smythyman, deputy controller of Philadelphia, discusses externally imposed constraints.

"Ten commandments" to motivate auditors are provided by the senior managing auditor of the Canadian Department of Supplies and Services, Paul J. Faulkner. Two articles on audit training describe the methods used by the progressive state audit operation in Wisconsin. They are by Daniel Frawley, administrator for training and research on the state auditor's staff. Robert L. Funk, former assistant director of the Municipal Finance Officers Association, tells how much knowledge of political science should be required for a qualified government audit staff.

Professional development for government auditors is reviewed by Albert I. Fox, assistant director for audit research, U.S. Department of the Interior. Donald L. Scantlebury, director of the U.S. General Accounting Office's Financial and General Management Studies Division, explains the use of consultants. This subject is expanded by

Paul Brubaker, former deputy auditor general of Pennsylvania and now with Coopers and Lybrand, in an article about planning for resource usage. Operating a quality assurance program as related to auditor evaluation is described by Edward Stepnick, director of the U.S. Department of Health, Education and Welfare's Audit Agency.

A case study on building a multidisciplined staff is given by Anthony Piccirilli, auditor general of Rhode Island, who organized the state's first legislative audit agency in 1975.

Personal Impairments — Their Impact on the Independence of the Government Auditor

E. William Rine, CIA

The Internal Auditor Sept./Oct. 1975

One of the general standards for governmental auditing is independence. The intent of this standard is to produce an environment wherein the audit staff may provide impartial opinions, conclusions, judgments, and recommendations. In order to accomplish this, the auditor must be completely free from any impairments restricting such independence.

Personal Impairments

Personal impairment is stated to be one of three impairments impacting upon independence. Six circumstances are listed in the standards as being related to personal impairments. For the most part, these circumstances relate to personal convictions or views. Of the six, two are less prevalent in an audit organization located within an operating or program agency such as the Law Enforcement Assistance Administration (LEAA). They are (1) financial interest, direct or indirect, in an organization or facility which is benefiting from the audited program and (2) actual or potential restrictive influence when the auditor performs preaudit work and subsequently performs a postaudit.

Preaudit work is minimal in LEAA and only relates to contract proposal audit assistance and providing financial data on prospective grantees. Our work is limited mostly to postauditing, management inspection, and investigation. Being in a government agency, the financial-interest element is not a critical factor. Most of our work involves state and local governments, and our auditing of profit or nonprofit corporations is minimal.

The other four circumstances defined in the standards as personal impairments could have a more direct impact on the LEAA auditor, even though the Office of Inspector General is independent of line authority and reports directly to the agency administrator. To some degree, these four circumstances are interrelated and, as such, should be treated together.

In order of importance, as they impact on the LEAA auditor, they are:

- Biases and prejudices, including those induced by political or social convictions, which result from employment in or loyalty to a particular group, entity, or level of government.
- Relationships of an official, professional, and/or personal nature that might cause the auditor to limit the extent or character of his inquiry, to limit disclosure, or to weaken his findings in any way.
- Previous involvement in a decision-making or management capacity in the operations of the governmental entity or program being audited.
- Preconceived ideas about the objectives or quality of a particular operation or personal likes or dislikes of individuals, groups, or objectives of a particular program.

Loyalty to the Agency

As a member of a government agency, we cannot imply an independence of position in the sense of absolute freedom from influence or, perhaps to some extent, control. As a LEAA auditor, we are part of the LEAA management team. As such, the auditor is no more independent than are the other members of the management team (program managers, comptroller, etc.). We are hired, paid, and directed (general in nature) by the administrator to perform certain functions. Since all employees normally have an ambition for personal success, achievement of that success requires the contribution of personal loyalty to and confidence of management as well as technical abilities. Therefore, being entirely human, the auditor is subject to the same influence as any other member of the management team.

An auditor is generally as independent as he wants to be. Thus, the auditor is in a unique position in that those qualities which are normally considered to be attributes may become the auditor's greatest obstacle. As part of the management team, the auditor should not go his merry own way independently of the actions, thinking, and direction of management. However, he should be factual and objective in reporting on activities.

Many of the sensitive situations we encounter are of management's own making. We must convince management of the true worth or nature of the activity. Sooner or later they will be disclosed, and we may be justly criticized for having passed up an opportunity to correct them. Therefore, the auditor should be factual and unbiased in calling management's attention to matters requiring corrective action, and these matters should be disclosed as early as possible.

The auditor must maintain his own independence of thinking and exploration. He should try to arrive at the facts and, after careful consideration, present them in such a manner that, even though they may be in conflict with present agency policies or thinking, they will be accepted and given due consideration.

The auditor has an obligation to exercise honesty, objectivity, and diligence in the performance of his duties and responsibilities. The amount of success attained depends a great deal on the integrity he demonstrates. He must exercise complete autonomy. However, the internal auditor, though acting independently, must have allegiance to the agency.

Day-to-Day Contacts with Management

Independence is not an attitude that remains uninfluenced by people and conditions; it must be cultivated and maintained. The auditor's day-to-day contacts with the management team could easily affect his appraisal. Personal familiarity with long-standing agency policies could lull the auditor into a false sense of trust. The auditor must maintain the best possible relations with the rest of the management team without sacrificing his own independence. Despite our best efforts to prevent such forces from affecting professional judgment, we must realize these influences are at work whether we are conscious of their effect or not. The auditor must maintain a mental balance which permits a constructive, critical analysis of the operations of the organization which is uninfluenced by personal loyalties.

The auditor, however great his personal integrity and independence of character, may always expect someone to question his opinion in his capacity of a staff member of the agency or as a result of association with members of the management team.

Biases and Preconceived Ideas

As a result of being a part of the management team and extremely close to the operations, the opportunity for preconceived opinions is great. Development of information to support a preconceived idea, ignoring facts which would weaken that preconception, is a lack of professional integrity. Integrity in an auditor is not merely a matter of honesty. The major test of his integrity is mental honesty. The auditor must assure himself that the findings he is reporting are, in his own mind, factual and above reproach.

Biased or preconceived ideas must never be permitted. We must never let personalities bias our judgment. We must develop facts – satisfactory and unsatisfactory alike – and throw both on the scales of judgment. Otherwise, we would lose our independence and, along with that, our integrity and honesty.

Independence, Ethics, and Open-mindedness Essential

Independence is what an auditor makes of his status. Without independence an audit may be considered as nothing more than a survey or staff paper. Independence used judiciously and coupled with personal integrity, honesty, and open-mindedness will assure high caliber auditing and reporting. This type of reporting will gain acceptance for all auditors by management, the management team, and all others having contact with the auditor. This acceptance exists within the LEAA.

External Influences Affecting the Independence of the Government Auditor

Jack Smithyman, CPA

The Internal Auditor Sept./Oct. 1975

Before we consider the subject of independence of the governmental auditor, we must first address the subject of independence of any auditor. Since we do not live in a utopia, it is unrealistic to assume any auditor can attain complete independence entirely free from influences of family, community, or the news he sees, hears, or reads – those external conflicts of interest that continually beset him.

Tom Higgins states in his article "Professional Ethics – A Time for Re-Appraisal" that a CPA has two kinds of independence: independence **in fact** and independence **in appearance.** The former refers to the person's objectivity and the latter, to his freedom from potential conflicts of interest. Inevitably, the auditor is confronted with these conflicts and must face them as he approaches a potential question of independence. To face these realities, the auditor should ask himself some basic questions as he approaches a potential question of independence:

- Will the relationship injure the interest of the public?
- Will the relationship affect his judgment?
- Will the relationship appear to a reasonable, prudent third party as one likely to sway the auditor's opinion?

The governmental auditor is confronted with several external influences that may affect his independence:

Political Pressures – One cannot deny that the governmental auditor is operating in a political environment. Concomitant are partisan considerations which may be a factor in seriously affecting the direction of the audit effort.

Financial Constraints – The auditor is susceptible to pressures from the funding source if he must appeal to the legislative or executive branch of government for operating funds. Therefore, he must have some independent right of appeal to be free of any scope restrictions that might be imposed because of the power to appropriate.

Legal Boundaries – Legislation or judicial decision can restrict the auditor in the type of audit he may make of the nature of the documents he may examine. This affects his investigative freedom and could limit his ability to determine where public money was spent and/or how efficiently and effectively resources (funds, personnel, facilities) were utilized.

Legislative and/or Executive Pressure – The legislative or executive branch can also place constraints, other than financial, on the auditor or place emphasis on the type or nature of the audit which would limit the auditor's digression.

SOCIOLOGICAL AND ECONOMIC FACTORS

Religious Affiliation/Natural Biases – Results of an audit of a governmental auditor are public knowledge; thus, the auditor is constantly working under public scrutiny. Consequently, there could be a restraining influence upon what he may or may not report on a particular segment of the community.

Credit Worthiness – Audit results have a major impact on the credit worthiness of the governmental unit. With this in mind, the governmental auditor may consider other approaches or methodology to arrive at an audit decision.

Period of Appointments – Short-term appointments have a disruptive effect upon the organization of the auditing unit because of the lack of continuity.

Federal and State Audit Agencies – Most federal and state agencies issue guidelines relative to the type of audit (compliance) appropriate to to the program funded. The funding agency may also set standards and procedures for other types of audits (e.g., program results).

Professional Groups – The auditor must adhere to rules, regulations, standards, procedures, and the like, of his professional organization. If, for example, he is a CPA, he must follow guidelines of both the state and the American Institute of Certified Public Accountants.

Organized Citizens Groups – He may be compelled to emphasize a particular audit program either because of direct pressures by these various groups or because of the results of their own investigations.

Subject to Independent Audit by Outside Groups – His agency may be audited by an independent accountant or other outside group either for its expenditures or for the quality of the audits performed.

Media – Pressures from the news media, as a result of letters to the editor, a special series of articles, or editorials, may be exerted upon the auditor for him to perform a particular audit or review. On the other hand, his credibility may be attacked by the media if they disagree with his reports.

Conflicts of Interest – He must scrupulously avoid all ties with previous firms or with personal clients that are affiliated with the governmental unit with which he now works.

In the end analysis, be it external influences, positions in the political organization, or any other factor, the only way that independence may be defined is "within the individual himself." It is his character and condition of mind, the human foundation, which is the cornerstone of independence.

How the City of Philadelphia Controller's Office Eliminated Some of the External Influences Which May Affect the Auditor's Independence

- The controller is elected by the people. This is mitigated by a short four-year term, although the controller may be reelected. It could also be mitigated by the ambitions of the office holder.
- The controller has direct access to the people and the press, and he reports all audit findings and recommendations to the people.
- Educational requirements of personnel performing audit functions are set down by the City Charter, which requires that the deputy in charge of audits be a CPA and that staff members be graduate accountants or CPA's.

- The City Charter requires that the auditor audit all operating funds in the city annually.
- The City Charter indicates that the controller is to review the economy and the efficiency of operations.
- Although the city controller must prepare budgets and submit these to the City Council and the mayor, the controller has the power to mandamus needed funds.
- Both the City Council and the mayor have the right to request special audit work. These requirements are over and above the requirements set down by the charter (to audit all operating funds of the city annually). Both the mayor and City Council have been very reasonable in their requests and have always justified their requests – and not merely for political reasons.
- Annually, the City Controller's Office has its annual budget appropriations audited by an independent CPA firm.
- Triennially, the City Council has the City Controller's Office reviewed on an operational basis by an independent CPA firm.

Motivating the Audit Staff

P. J. Faulkner

The Internal Auditor Jan./Feb. 1976

History is replete with examples of listings of do's and don'ts. Although taking many forms, they were all designed as guides for individual conduct. Probably, the most famous such listing is the Ten Commandments.

At the risk of proliferation and with due respect to the past eminent lawgivers, one more list of do's and don'ts is offered. These guidelines are offered to the audit manager. If followed, they should assist him/her in the difficult task of motivating the audit staff. These guidelines cannot claim the inspiration of others that have gone before them, yet they can claim the cement of practical experience. Their application has worked.

Accordingly, hereunder are the ten commandments to be followed by the audit manager in order to motivate the audit staff:

1. *Thou shalt always be honest, truthful, and straightforward with thy staff.* This is the first and greatest commandment upon which all the others must rest. Unless the manager shows sin-

cerity and integrity in dealing with the audit staff, there can be no motivation of these people towards fulfilling the objectives of the audit group. Without mutual trust, any other good efforts of the audit manager will be like a seed falling upon barren ground.

2. *Thou shalt not keep thy people in the dark.* By reason of position in the organization's hierarchy, the audit manager is cognizant of the policies, plans, and direction of the organization. This kind of information must be considered vital to motivation; it is also necessary in order that the auditors can perform their evaluations in a truly effective manner.
3. *Thou shalt provide for the participation of thy staff in managing the audit function.* To truly motivate a professional group such as auditors, they must be allowed to participate in the management of the function. Their ideas and input should be sought in matters of audit policy. Too, they should be permitted to input their ideas into the terms of reference and timing of any audit assignment.
4. *Thou shalt provide a forum for the exchange of ideas between staff members.* In addition to allowing participation in management, the audit manager should allow and encourage intragroup communication. A free exchange of ideas within the audit group would not only help motivate the individuals of the group but could also raise the effectiveness of the audit function itself.
5. *Thy audit reports must reflect an effective and professional group.* The audit report, the final output of the audit group, must be well packaged. For those who receive it, the report is the mirror image of the audit group. The report should be well formatted, well typed, well written, and well presented. One cannot expect any feeling of pride within the audit group when a poorly presented report is given to management.
6. *Thou shalt not nitpick thy auditors' reports.* Satisfy yourself that the required message is clearly stated in the report. Nothing will demoralize an author faster than the editor who must nitpick at individual words and phrases. Provide the auditor with some pride of authorship. Let the auditor's name appear on the report and let the words in that report be those of the auditor.
7. *Thou must control the activities of thy staff.* While the third commandment provides for participation by the audit group in the management of the audit function, it does not relieve the audit manager of the responsibility to control. The manager still has this responsibility and must exercise it. A management-by-results program in the audit organization could be used effectively to motivate the staff to achieve agreed-to results.
8. *Thou shalt provide for the training of thy staff.* Adequate provision must be made for the training and professional development of the audit staff. They are, after all, a group of professionals. The audit manager should not only provide for training and development; but, indeed, they should be encouraged!
9. *Thou shalt provide for the career development of thy staff.* To motivate the audit staff, some reasonably clear patterns for personal and professional growth

should be apparent to them. Promotion opportunities should be available to those who merit them. Not only plans but some record of achievement of these plans should be visible to the members of the audit group. Opportunities should be available within the audit group itself and within the organization that it serves.

10. *Thou shalt make thy audit program effective. The effectiveness* of the audit function will measure the motivation of the audit staff. An audit that provides meaningful information to management so that management are prepared to act upon the recommendations of the auditor is not only an effective management tool but is also a vital motivation for the audit staff. There can be no motivation if the auditor feels that his efforts are in vain.

Although these ten commandments for the audit manager are not engraved in stone nor written in Sanskrit, they wil be useful in motivating the audit staff. These people are professionals in every sense of the word, but they are human too. They are engaged in a difficult and often unappreciated task. To get the most out of them and to fully reap the advantages of their professionalism is, perhaps, the major challenge facing the audit manager. These guidelines are offered in the hope that their use will help in motivating auditors.

State Audit Staff Training

Daniel D. Frawley, CPA

The Internal Auditor Mar./April 1973

A major concern of all employers, governmental units as well as private industry, is the training of audit staffs. I believe we can accept the assurance of most accounting faculty members that auditing is the hardest subject to teach the accounting undergraduate. In that sense they are referring mainly to financial audit. With the present emphasis on operational auditing to augment financial auditing in state government, the educational background and capability of a competent operational auditor must go beyond the requirements of financial auditors. As state auditors, devoting more and more of our limited auditing hours to operational audit, we do not have established guidelines such as the A.P.B. opinions or statements to rely on. We do not have the statements on auditing procedure as a Bible; neither do we have the Internal Revenue code or SEC regulations as basic source information. We must develop staff that can rely on skill and common sense rather than checklists or manuals.

To train our members we have a number of sources to which we look for help. They can be identified as follows: (1) on the job training, (2) Cadmus Education Foundation courses, (3) American Management Association courses, (4) federal government courses, (5) university courses, (6) private specialty contract courses, (6) in-house courses, (7) Wisconsin State CPA courses, (8) Council of State Government courses, and (9) attendance at professional meetings and conventions.

Another major element in our training program is a fairly extensive reading collection consisting of about 500 current books dealing with most aspects of accounting, auditing, mathematics, economics, management, motivation and state and federal audit requirements. Most of our EDP material is maintained in loose-leaf type services in view of the rapid changes in this area. A rapid count shows that we receive some 60 periodicals and journals ranging from specialty magazines dealing largely with single subjects such as personnel, hospitals, colleges and universities to general publications of interest to all auditors, accountants, and managers. Our subscriptions are constantly reviewed to make sure that our staff can understand and will take the time to read the various publications.

Beyond these subscriptions, we make extensive use of reports issued by the General Accounting Office, The Rand Corporation, The Institute of Internal Auditors, Inc., The Committee for Economic Development and publications of many of the larger CPA firms.

Another phase of our training program is a fair amount of pressure placed on the staff to join and actively participate in professional organizations.

Membership in these various groups (which is paid by the individual) is encouraged to avoid parochialism on our part. We believe that our members must have access to the most current thinking in operational audit and not attempt to continually reinvent the wheel. We need a staff that has the background to design a better tire for the wheel.

Basically we believe that there are certain general considerations that must be considered and evaluated before any audit training program can be set up. These are:

A. Funds available for training
B. Personnel
    1. People we have on staff
        a. Basic education
        b. Past experience
        c. Fields of special interest
    2. What we need
C. Economics
    1. Salary ranges and fringe benefits must be competitive.
    2. Advancement opportunities must be available as a result of improved performance resulting from staff training.
D. Generally don't invest money in training that will not be used soon.

With these basics once settled we can then turn to the questions of how to train the individual as well as the entire staff so as to maximize our limited resources. Although Wisconsin may not be typical, we have a full time research and training administrator whose major duties include recruiting and coordinating training and research. The next installment will present more specific management aspects on training.

Audit Training in the Wisconsin Legislative Audit Bureau

Daniel D. Frawley, CPA

The Internal Auditor May/June 1973

Maximum utilization of assets, establishment of maximum attainable goals, supervision and motivation are the cornerstones of management. We have found that our new staff members – college graduates with accounting majors – have satisfactory backgrounds in most technical areas. They also have some knowledge of EDP and a concept of financial audit. However, their greatest weakness appears to be in the behavioral sciences and a lack of knowledge of managerial concepts.

A review of the college transcripts of new graduates generally shows a certain sameness: 18 to 24 credits in accounting, 10 to 12 hours in some type of economics, business law and some mathematic courses. A few transcripts will show variations. Hopefully, you will find some with more than average English and psychology credits or one who has had more than an introductory management course.

To develop these members into good auditors is not an overnight task. We are faced with the limitations imposed on most state central governmental audit agencies. Salary ranges, lack of profit centers in government, combination financial and operational audits, and a continual manpower shortage are among the factors contributing to our problems.

Within this framework we attempt to develop competent operational auditors. On-the-job training is the keystone of our program. Our performance ratings at the end of each audit show what each auditor on the audit did and in which areas he needs training. The supervisor preparing the rating suggests formal training courses and adds general information for the next auditor-in-charge on which areas the new auditor needs experience.

Writing courses have been taken by 90% of the staff. The Institute's courses in operational auditing and advanced staff auditor's development have been taken by many. Technical courses ranging from EDP audit, statistical mathematics,

PERT/CPM to the auditing of specific federal programs have been taken by most of our staff. Through these courses and others, we have generally given our personnel adequate technical knowledge.

The problem of developing a knowledgeable management talent and attitude within the staff is not as simple. It can be as basic as the sign in many audit offices, *"WHY,"* or as complex as the many texts that we have in our library on the subject of management.

Among the techniques we have found valuable are the monthly staff meetings where four or five of the newer staff members explain and defend any management or legislative change that may be recommended in the audit they are currently working on. Under cross examination by their peers on the staff, they develop not only experience in facing groups and thinking on their feet, but more importantly, they develop the ability to fully analyze and defend audit recommendations they or their co-workers are proposing.

On-the-job training ideally starts with letting the newer members participate in formulating the audit program so they can see what areas are to be covered in the audit, the purpose of the audit and their contribution to the audit.

Most audits can be fragmented into segments that do not require one auditor spending the entire period operating an adding machine or a calculator. We attempt to give a member an auditor's job on each audit and not utilize him for his first year as a clerk. Development of his analytical talent and hopefully his management potential starts with this first audit assignment.

Our audit directors, supervisors and auditors-in-charge are constantly questioned and reminded that the development of the newer members under their charge is one of the primary functions of their job.

The audit segments assigned to all staff members are hopefully within their capabilities. We want everyone to keep breathing, but yet to swim to the best of their ability. This constant challenge seems to motivate them to do their best, and to insure their rapid development as operational auditors and managers.

By the rules of our state personnel board we are required to list certain job openings on a statewide basis. The best proof of State Auditor Ringwood's "Motivation by Challenge" policy can be shown by the number of state employees who are willing to transfer to the Legislative Audit Bureau without an increase in salary or even at a reduced grade. In turn, the auditors who leave our staff seem to leave only for clear-cut major promotions in positions generally within our state government.

The Qualified Government Audit Staff: How Much Political Science?

Robert L. Funk

The Internal Auditor May/June 1975

The growing emphasis placed on program and management audits in the government sector underscores a basic standard:

> **The auditors assigned to perform the audit must collectively possess adequate professional proficiency for the tasks required.**[1]

Implicit in this criterion is that the auditor have an adequate knowledge of the "environment" within which the audit is to be conducted. Within the private sector, this requires the auditor to have a knowledge of business law, economics, finance, and an understanding of the business entity in its diversity of forms and organizations as well as of accounting and auditing. More often than not, emphasis has been on accounting and auditing.

This is recognized by virtually all of those concerned with the auditor and his background. For example, Carey states: "The CPA firm will have to look at a client's business as a whole – much as a competent physician examines the whole patient before diagnosing or prescribing for a local ailment."[2] The need for a thorough understanding of the total environment was also noted by Campfield:

> **It is abundantly clear that the domain of the management auditor embraces a wide spectrum of organization plans, processes, and problems. To render effective service, a management auditor must have substantial knowledge of the total environment of the organization he examines.**[3]

Knowledge and Training Required

It is apparent that, if the auditor is to have knowledge of the environment within which he is to apply his skills, he must have a broad, general liberal arts education. Some of this educational background may be obtained in general courses such as economics and the behavioral sciences that have equal applicability to both the private and public sectors. Some of the tools that will be required may be applied equally in both sectors such as training in the application of the "scientific" method and in research methodology, statistics, data analysis, and mathematics.

It is also apparent that, if the auditor working in the governmental sector is to have a knowledge of the environment within which he works, he must augment the background training and education that may apply to either the public or private sector with some training that relates specifically to government. This will require basic courses in political science and its related subfield of public administration.

---

[1]General Accounting Office, *Standards for Audit of Governmental Organizations, Programs, Activities and Functions,* General Accounting Office, p. 6.

[2]John L. Carey, *The CPA Plans for the Future,* American Institute of Certified Public Accountants, New York.

[3]William L. Campfield, "Education for Management Auditing," *The Federal Accountant* (Spring 1966): 33.

There is no consensus as to the amount of training in political science that is desirable. This will depend upon the size of the audit staff. If sufficiently large and specialization can be achieved, it may well be that a graduate with a major in political science should form part of the team. His expertise in government would be balanced by those with specialties in finance, industrial engineering, accounting, etc. In this respect, it may be noted that the present comptroller general of the United States has a PhD in political science and that several of those heading major state or county audit staffs also have majored in this discipline.

The Minimum Requirements

As a minimum, an auditor in the government sector should have sufficient exposure in political science to understand governmental institutions, their operation, and the factors that affect them. Courses in American government, state and local government, political philosophy, political policy, public finance and the budgetary process, and administrative law would give the governmental auditor the prerequisite background to better understand the environment within which he is conducting his audit. This would certainly sharpen his ability to conduct the type of audit that would be most beneficial to all concerned in achieving the three "E's" applicable to the government as a whole or to any of its programs: efficiency, effectiveness, and economy. Such a background would also aid in preparing an audit report and directing its commentary in a way so as to enhance the implementation of the recommendations.

Professional Development — A Progressive Policy for Interior's Auditors

Albert I. Fox, CPA

The Internal Auditor Sept./Oct. 1973

The Audit Operations office of the U.S. Department of the Interior has an interesting and forward-looking professional development policy for its 125 auditors.

Through its headquarters and three regional offices, Audit Operations performs operational audits of the more than 20 bureaus and major offices that comprise the Interior Department (such as the National Park Service, Bureau of Indian Affairs, Geological Survey, Bureau of Reclamation and Bonneville Power Administration). It also audits the Interior's contractors and grantees.

The Policy

A number of Federal agencies and other organizations have shown much interest in the policy on professional development published by Audit Operations.

The policy envisions a cooperative effort among the auditor, his (or her) supervisors, and a headquarters official in designing a one-year and longer-range plan for the auditor. The plan considers not only the types of training contemplated in the published policy for the auditor's salary level, but also considers his particuar training needs and objectives.

The recommendations of his supervisors, his education, previous training and experience, and his personal interests and career goals, are important in designing the plan. His supervisors provide input by commenting on his performance and recommending areas of training in a professional staff appraisal prepared semi-annually. His career profile – summarizing his principal academic subjects, achievements, professional employment record and training – is also carefully studied.

The Objective

The essential objective of the policy is to foster the continuing professional development of the auditor, advising and assisting him in advancing his knowledge and auditing capabilities for the mutual benefit of the office and himself. In achieving the objective, the office schedules his attendance at officially - sponsored training courses. It also assists by providing generous financial incentives for his own professional development efforts.

The Procedure

The Interior pays the full cost for auditors it enrolls in professional society meetings and symposiums, seminars and other training sessions. For business-related college or other courses the auditor desires to study in pursuing his own professional development program (usually outside of regular duty hours), the Interior ordinarily shares, but may pay up to, the full cost.

The extent to which the Interior participates financially depends on the degree it decides the office or department will benefit. It further considers the benefit the auditor is likely to gain personally from the training. In most instances, the Interior believes there are advantages in having the auditor share in defraying the cost of a self-development course he selects.

If the auditor desires to take a review course in preparing for the CPA examination, the Interior pays half the cost. The auditor is also granted time to sit for the examination, including essential travel time, without charge to annual leave. An interesting recent change in the policy removed a limit of $150 as the Interior's share of the cost of a CPA review course but retained the limit of one-half. Further, the Interior now pays or shares in the cost of prescribed books and supplies, as well as the tuition for any course it approves. Previously, the interior's share was based on tuition costs only.

A further important change in the policy related to the timing of payment by the Interior. Instead of paying the agreed amount to the training institution when the auditor enrolls, the Interior now reimburses the auditor when he satisfactorily completes a course. This change avoids problems which could arise if the auditor did not complete the course after the Interior paid its share. However, the auditor still must obtain the Interior's advance approval for the course. To obtain reimbursement, the auditor submits a letter or certificate attesting to the completion and copies of cancelled checks or other receipts.

If the Interior agrees to participate financially in a course presented by a non-Federal facility, the auditor must agree to continue serving in the Federal Government for at least three times the length (hours) of the course. He is not required to sign the agreement, however, if the course includes less than 80 hours of classroom instruction or is a correspondence course.

The policy is readily adaptable to assist the auditor in meeting his continuing education requirements. These requirements for Federal accountants and auditors, patterned on pronouncements of the AICPA for Certified Public Accountants, are being studied by the Federal Government Accountants Association.

The Interior's professional develoment policy has been effective in planning and coordinating the auditor's training and in encouraging his own professional development efforts. Numerous auditors have availed themselves of the opportunity afforded under the policy to advance their accounting and auditing education.

The Use of Consultants

Donald L. Scantlebury, CIA, CPA

The Internal Auditor May/June 1975

The extension of the work of the auditor beyond the realm of accounting has created many problems for auditors. In the old days when an auditor could confine himself to accounting matters, he had the expertise he needed to do his job if he understood accounting well and had an elementary knowledge of commercial law. The extension of his work into what is often referred to as "operational" or "performance auditing" has made demands upon him for skills in a wide number of additional fields of knowledge, including engineering, statistics, advanced mathematics, and medicine. Obviously, it is not practical for an auditor to try to equip himself with knowledge in all these fields. Life is too short. He must therefore seek other ways of acquiring the needed knowledge.

In the General Accounting Office, we have found that the best way to acquire the needed skills is to hire experts in these areas — such as for instance, an engineer or a statistician and let them work with the auditors. This is only practical, of course, when there is sufficient need for the services of the expert to make it worthwhile to employ him full time. In many cases, this will not be practical and the auditor with a particular audit problem calling for skills he does not have must, therefore, turn to experts that are not on his staff.

The use of such experts presents a host of new problems to the auditor: How do you find them? What is the best way to pay them for their services? How will you evaluate their work?

From my experiences in using such experts in the General Accounting Office, I offer some suggestions for dealing with these problems:

Where Do I Find the Consultants?

Universities are often good sources of consultants. They have professors who are highly specialized in a variety of different fields. Moreover, they are often able to adjust their schedules to do consulting work. In some fields there are professional consulting firms that can be employed. Too, professional societies are often good sources for finding qualified consultants. They may often direct you to a number of firms or individuals who are qualified and interested in short-term consulting work.

How Should I Pay Them?

Probably, a fixed fee for the job is the best way if the auditor can be specific enough about what he wants done. If he is not, a not uncommon situation, we have found the use of a basic per-diem rate permits flexibility and may promote competition among qualified consultants if several are available.

How Will You Evaluate Their Work?

We have found that consultants can often explain what they have done clearly enough so that the auditor can draw his own conclusions as to the acceptability of their work. When this is not possible, we have used another expert or a panel to obtain an opinion.

Other Suggestions

While we have generally had success in the use of consultants, there are some important lessons we have learned. These are:

- Do not let the experts work alone. They often get sidetracked by things that interest them but which are not pertinent to the audit. See that an auditor keeps in constant touch with them to see that they stay on the subject.
- Do not rely on them to understand auditors' needs for documentation. Most other professions do not document their work as well as auditors, so it is desirable to have their papers reviewed frequently and carefully.
- Be prepared to help them translate what they have done into simple English. Many of them will have had little experience in writing for a nontechnical audience and will need help here.

With a few basic rules like those cited above to guide him, an auditor can secure help from outside experts that will considerably broaden his ability to do effective audit work.

Managing the Audit — Planning For Resource Usage

Paul Brubaker, Jr.

The Internal Auditor Jan./Feb. 1976

Planning for the use of manpower in an audit usually translates into time represented by dollar cost. Most audit agencies have fixed budgets of dollars that will buy a limited number of man-hours broken down among managers, supervisors, and staff. Audit planning may represent a compromise between what we would like to do versus what can be accomplished with the resources available.

In the case of financial audits, staff resources may be spread over the required audit work to achieve the objective of reviewing financial information and rendering an opinion of financial statements. With the advent of the concepts of auditing efficiency, economy, and program results, we have a different problem.

We may now find that our resources in the form of financial auditors are limited and of dubious worth in analyzing a medical or social program. In order to do comprehensive program audits, we must find and allocate special resources. Essentially, there are three choices:

- Hire persons from disciplines other than accounting and auditing
- Retrain financial auditors
- Engage consultants to assist in the program review audits in special areas

There is a tendency for auditing agencies to seek out special talents other than accounting when looking for new employees, but this trend has developed slowly. Several problems exist with this approach. First, there must be sufficient lead time to work these persons into the audit staff. In other words, the need for special talents must be anticipated well in advance. Once these specialized talents are available, they must be utilized on a continuing basis.

Another alternative is to develop specialists from the regular audit staff. This means an additional training cost to the agency and time lost in performing audits.

The third alternative is to hire special consultants on an "as-needed" or limited basis. This alternative is the most flexible and should result in lower dollar costs since some special talents will only be needed infrequently for limited periods of time.

The balance of this article will discuss several cases of the use of independent consultants in widely different disciplines. One of the most interesting parts of the experience is locating and evaluating these consultants.

Treasury Department

When the Pennsylvania Department of the Auditor General wanted to review the investment procedures and cash management function of the State Treasurer's Department, there was a need for specialized expertise, not found on the regular staff. The department could not use a bank or investment house presently dealing with the state because they would not be independent.

The department did not have the time nor the money to hire additional full-time staff specialists. We decided to engage an investment counselor and a former commercial banker to assist us for a period of several months. They found that invested funds were not earning sufficient return and that many millions of dollars that could have been invested were not invested.

In addition, several millions of dollars of bank balances were not properly collateralized. They also found a disproportionate amount of dollars invested in unsecured commercial paper. The Treasury Department was trying to maintain a multibillion dollar investment program with a limited staff advised by several major Pennsylvania banks that obviously put their own interests foremost.

State Employees Retirement Fund

In the case of the State Employees Retirement Fund, financial audits were conducted using strictly financial auditing techniques. These audits were several years late historically because of the lack of systems and EDP capability at the Fund. After the Fund retained an independent CPA firm to design and implement an EDP system, it was possible to get current information for the first time.

Unfortunately, the average auditor does not know how to evaluate actuarial data. Even though the Fund had retained a consulting actuary over the years, their primary concern was to come up with the actuarial valuation annually.

It was decided to retain independent consulting actuaries to analyze available data. From these data, a report was prepared commenting on the benefit structure, financing basis, investment review, administrative procedures, and suggested legislative changes. This part of the report could not have been prepared without the help of the pension actuaries and investment counsel referred to above.

Other Specialized Resources

The many activities of government suggest additional areas where specialized resources are needed. Some of these are related to financial information, but many are not. The department, when confronted by an analysis of coal miners' black-lung claims, sought the services of a casualty actuary. In auditing the highway fund, the use of independent engineers should be helpful. Perhaps, the two most difficult areas to examine are medical and educational; but these areas can also be evaluated by appropriate professional personnel retained by the auditing agency.

The Quality Assurance Program — Auditing the Auditor

Edward Stepnick

The Internal Auditor Jan./Feb. 1976

Franklin Pinkelman, Michigan's deputy auditor general, discussed (July/August 1975 issue) ways to assure overall quality of audit work and reporting when the work was being done.

We would like to discuss one way the HEW Audit Agency tests the effectiveness of its audit process. We call it the "Quality Assurance Program." It is challenging, interesting, and rewarding.

We kicked the program off in January of 1973 with our first review at our Atlanta regional audit office. However, it goes back even further when considering the time spent in developing and planning the approach and techniques. In discussing our approach to planning and conducting these reviews and what happens when we report the results, perhaps we will spur others who may be thinking of implementing a similar program.

The HEW Audit Agency is organized with a headquarters group in Washington, D.C., and ten regional offices throughout the United States. Including branch offices and suboffices, we have staffs at over 50 locations, thus providing opportunities for plenty of variations — good and bad — from prescribed norms. Thus far, our reviews have concentrated on regional and related branch offices. Eventually, all the audit agency's locations will be covered.

Planning the Review

Proper planning is the keystone to the success of quality assurance reviews. Planning involves the selection of a review staff; review of organizational, background, and productivity data of each entity selected for review; and preparation of a review guide (e.g., audit program). As for staffing, our reviews to date show best results with a mix of Audit Agency headquarters' staff and regional staff selected from other than the office under review. The size of the review team varies, depending on the geographical makeup of the region. We find that three or four can do a thorough review in three weeks or so.

Team members should meet certain qualifications: a reputation for professionalism, good interpersonal skills, and sound analytical ability. To assure an experienced team leader and to provide program continuity, one of the headquarters' divisions supplies key team members on each review. Once the staff is selected, but prior to the fieldwork, the final planning step must be performed: preparation of a quality assurance review guide specifically tailored to the entity to be reviewed.

Quality Assurance Review Guide

Our quality assurance review guides are divided into three major segments, calling for detailed review of:

- The organizational setup of regional components, including methods followed in allocating resources and planning work load requirements
- Audit management techniques over work performance, includ-

ing tests of the timeliness and quality of individual audit reports

- Miscellaneous administrative and support activities.

Briefly, the review objectives are to judge whether the audit component has marshalled its resources in a manner that will best accomplish its mission; to see if the audit staff follows prescribed auditing standards, policies, and procedures; and to consider the adequacy of administrative and other support activities. Although the criteria are still quite judgmental in some areas, we find that adherence to the review guide will not only provide a satisfactory appraisal but will also lead to constructive recommendations for improvements.

Reporting Procedures

The results of each quality assurance review are carefully pulled together in a narrative report addressed to the regional audit director whose office was reviewed.

The report looks like a typical internal audit report. It discusses the observations and findings of the review team and recommendations for corrective action. Prior to the final report, however, the team goes over its work with appropriate regional audit staff; and an exit conference provides an opportunity for any disagreements to be ironed out. Also, a draft copy of the report is provided for comment before it is finalized.

In transmitting the final report, the director of the HEW Audit Agency asks for a plan of action on the recommended corrective measures and follows up personally to see that important matters are satisfactorily resolved. The entire process is handled without fuss or favor. Thanks to the quality of the review teams, divisiveness and abrasiveness have been avoided.

Planning Is Needed for Success

In summary, the Quality Assurance Program is designed to aid responsible audit officials in seeing how well the audit function is carried out. Proper planning, including good staffing and a detailed review guide, is important to the success of each review. Each review may be completed in a short time with worthwhile benefits in improving the quality of audits and achieving better manpower utilization.

Developing a Legislative Audit Agency In Rhode Island

Anthony Piccirilli, CPA

The Internal Auditor May/June 1975

In 1974 Rhode Island joined the majority of states which have legislative audit agencies. We were faced with both the challenge and the opportunity of building a productive audit operation from the ground up. These remarks are meant to outline the approach we used in creating an audit agency staff and, hopefully, to help others who may be confronted with the same problem.

Building a Legislative Audit Organization

The legislation that created the Rhode Island Office of the Auditor General placed this legislative audit agency under the authority of the General Assembly's Joint Committee on Legislative Affairs. Based on this legislation, the Committee is given the power to "employ qualified persons necessary for the efficient operation of the office and shall fix their duties and compensation." By evaluating what is and should be expected of us, a staff is selected which possesses the disciplines necessary to accomplish those tasks. The nature and extent of future audits by this agency will be determined by the dictates of our legal mandate which requires us, upon approval of the Committee, to perform "postaudits and performance audits of accounts and records of all state agencies, public body or political subdivisions or any association or corporation created by any general or special law of the General Assembly, or any person, association, or corporation to which monies of the state have been appropriated by the General Assembly."

In order to properly discharge our responsibility, it was mandatory that the body of auditors selected possess the needed experience to meet the broad range of operational audits to be performed. With this requisite in mind, auditors with varied experience and expertise were selected. Their background included governmental auditing while associated with public accounting firms, internal auditing within the federal government, and considerable exposure to the private industrial sector both in the areas of auditing and financial management with an international accounting firm. This group of five accounting professionals, of which four are certified public accountants, provides our agency with a solid core of audit competence and experience.

Even with this wide range of experience, a great deal of initial staff time was expended in staff meetings to develop quality control and our own audit procedures and techniques which would embrace both the American Institute of Certified Public Accountants' (AICPA) and GAO's auditing standards.

We have encouraged participation in AICPA activities and intragovernmental seminars and training workshops. Most staff members are enrolled in voluntary continuing education programs sponsored by the Rhode Island Society of Certified Public Accountants.

Staff Members Outside the Accounting Profession

The scope of legislative audits in Rhode Island expands beyond the traditional financial examination to include performance audits. This broader audit definition requires the use of specialized expertise. In anticipating the need for this necessary knowledge and expertise, we hired the specialists necessary to accomplish this broadened scope. Our present specialists provide expertise in (1) financial analysis, (2) governmental research, and (3) computer systems analysis to our audit organization. This group adds a great deal to the agency's professional proficiency in that it enforces our ability to deliver comprehensive evaluations of government programs.

The Financial Analyst

The appointment of a financial analyst filled the need for special analytical skills. Bringing in an experienced financial analyst from the business world enabled the audit agency to utilize the traditional tools of financial analysis long used in industry planning and management and which are equally applicable to government.

The role of the financial analyst has been to make use of facts and situations developed during an audit which require further evaluation in order to determine their impact on governmental operations. As a result, the evaluations furnished by the financial analyst can be integrated with the results of the audit to provide more comprehensive and meaningful audit reports.

In addition to this input during audits, the financial analyst also is assigned special studies as the result of specific requests directed to the auditor general by the legislature.

The Research Analyst

The research analyst has training in public administration and experience both in government and with a private research agency evaluating governmental functions. He brought a knowledge of government to our audit agency that has proved helpful in the orientation of the staff to the structure of our state government. The researcher's special contributions to the staff were a background of how government was operating in terms of programs and personnel which helps the audit staff to "dig out" the facts about program operations and experience in survey research useful in the preliminary stage of audits.

The Systems Analyst

The systems analyst strengthened our staff in an area of expanding government activity: the growing dependence on electronic data processing (EDP) in many agencies of government.

Auditing in a computer environment requires special staff skills, and having a computer specialist on staff gives our legislative audit team these required skills.

It must be kept in mind that, if an agency uses EDP in its accounting system – whether the application is simple or complex – the auditor needs to understand the entire system sufficiently to allow him to recognize essential accounting control features. The Rhode Island State government uses EDP applications extensively. For example, the semiannual audit of our state lottery, which entails a complex EDP system, requires that an individual trained and experienced in computer science assist in this audit. The systems analyst has the technical training and proficiency necessary to provide the necessary assistance to the auditor in understanding these automated areas in the accounting system.

This individual has extensive training and experience in the methods and applications of computer technology. He has had experience as a programmer and systems analyst and was responsible for directing a data processing department in private industry.

More specialists may be required in the years ahead, but we have made initial staff additions only in those areas of expertise most needed during our early operations. An option open to us in the future is the use of consultant specialists to be engaged as needed rather than adding permanent staff members.

We recognize that disciplines in addition to accountancy are required to obtain our objectives, and we are committed to obtaining experts in the necessary disciplines either as staff additions or by specific engagements.

7
audit operations

Any discussion of audit operations contains what governmental auditing is all about. The audit standards developed by the GAO covered this area under the standard for due professional care and the five standards of the Examination and Evaluation group. The subjects vary from planning and supervising to the optimum characteristics for audit evidence.

Planning the audit operation includes not only the identification of the audits to be conducted but also planning the audit staff operations and the time to be used. If audits are conducted by several teams, planning must coordinate the work of the teams so that data collected are comparable and can be woven into a single report. Planning includes attention to anticipated interim and fiscal reporting.

In identifying the audits to be conducted, the audit director sets priorities. The criteria that can be used include such items as: (1) the dollar amount of a program; (2) the risk involved relative to potential loss; (3) sensitive programs in social, political, and economic areas; (4) legislative interest; (5) newness of programs; and (6) programs reported as needing attention.

At this point, the audit schedule and the planning can be converted into a budget for executive or legislative review and approval.

The first thing done on an audit is the preparation of an audit guide. This guide, which includes the parameters within which the audit will be conducted, contains background information and the general plans for the audit, including an outline for resource usage, timetables, an outline or digest of the audit report, a plan for control and quality evaluation, and an outline for scheduled conferences with client and auditee groups.

The preliminary survey is a device that is time-tested and cost-beneficial. A well-planned preliminary survey includes a review of all pertinent documentation including earlier audit reports; interviews with officials and workers; a walk-through inspection to examine inventories, facilities, and layout; and a survey report. The report summarizes the entire process and identifies the areas that should be examined in detail or indicates where audit work will be reduced. As a result of the survey, the audit staff is able to concentrate on areas that appear to have considerable payoff potential. This assures the development of an efficient audit program.

The program contains information on the thrust of the audit, its objective, the general methodology to be used, and areas to be covered. The intended purpose for each area of audit effort should be specified. Procedure and depth of detail for testing should be left to the audit team.

The use of sampling and computers in conducting audits has become quite commonplace. Most audit staffs include specialists in both of these areas. The techniques of audit testing include setting standards, defining populations, selecting samples, and examining transactions through observing, questioning, analyzing, verifying, investigating, and evaluating.

The audit of operations includes more of a survey and operations analysis technique than a detailed testing of transactions. Analytical processes resulting in flowcharts, organization charts, and narrative comments are more common than testing schedules. Compliance with prescribed procedures and comparisons of operations to good business practices, to logical organizational checks and structure, and to established performance standards become important elements in the audit process.

Finally, the use of working papers and the development of evidence serve to document the audit work and its results. They also serve as the basis of reports and to provide backup support if items in the audit report are questioned or are the object of litigation.

The articles in this chapter address themselves to nearly all these operational elements. The first article by Dr. Walter L. Johnson, assistant professor of the University of Missouri, discusses audit programs and guides. The second article, by Allan L. Reynolds, director of audit and investigation of the U.S. Department of the Interior, provides some interesting insight on the audit survey. The consideration of priorities in scheduling audits is addressed by Daniel D. Frawley, administrator of research and training on the staff of Wisconsin's state auditor. Ben Robinson, assistant director (U.S. Department of Agriculture, Office of Audit), discusses the synergetic effect of using the audits of others to fulfill audit responsibility.

The subject of computer auditing as an integral and essential part of governmental audit is described by Robert V. Graham, state auditor (Washington). William Wilkerson, Chief Advanced Techniques Staff, U.S. Department of Health, Education and Welfare, Audit Agency, expands the subject to cover the integration of the statistical approach.

Quality control of audit effort and reporting is covered in an article by Deputy Auditor General Franklin C. Pinkelman of Michigan. Daniel D. Frawley provides another article on evaluating the effectiveness of the audit operation, and three articles describe evidence. Edward P. Chait, an audit manager of Price Waterhouse & Co., covers sufficiency. Dr. T. Arthur Smith, director of education of the Association of Government Accountants, discusses reliability; and Dr. Herbert A. O'Keefe, Jr., professor of accounting of Savannah State College (Georgia), treats evidence and relevance. The discussion of the subject concludes with an article on permanent file material by County Auditor Grady Fullerton (Harris County, Texas).

The final article in this chapter covers audits in Michigan counties. It was written by the state's assistant treasurer, James J. Bolthouse.

Audit Programs and Guides — Is There a Difference?

Dr. Walter L. Johnson, CPA

The Internal Auditor July/Aug. 1975

Auditing, like many other emergent disciplines, occasionally is afflicted with a certain imprecision about some of its basic terms. While on first thought, for example, it would seem that everyone understands the difference between an audit guide and an audit program, nowhere in the literature is a distinction between the two terms clearly drawn.

Audit Programs

Most audit practitioners, especially those schooled as CPA's, would probably define an audit program in words like these written by R. K. Mautz in *Fundamentals of Auditing:*

An audit program consists of a series of verification procedures to be applied to the financial statements and accounts of a given company for the purpose of obtaining sufficient competent evidential matter so the auditor can express an informed opinion about the fairness of presentation of the financial statements or other data he has examined.

The audit program serves two main purposes: First, it serves as a "plan of attack on the particular verification problem at hand; second, it serves as a record of the work performed during the audit," according to Mautz. Moreover, an audit program is essential as a means of coordinating complex audits and for effecting communication between members of an audit team. In short, the audit program constitutes the embodiment of generally accepted auditing fieldwork standards elaborated and applied to particular circumstances.

In passing, we may note that not all authorities agree on the degree of detail with which audit programs should outline verification procedures. Mautz says: "The program should state specifically what is to be done," adding such statements as: "Foot and crossfoot the cash receipts book for the month of December and trace all postings to the general ledger."

Lawrence B. Sawyer's view differs from Mautz's. True, Sawyer describes an audit program as a "plan of action for an audit examination" in his book *The Practice of Modern Internal Auditing;* and by itself, this differs little from Mautz's description. But Sawyer goes on to say: "The program provides guidelines and does not set forth detailed audit steps." "Those steps," he suggests, "will be listed in the scope sections of the working papers dealing with the individual audit segments."

No matter what one's view is concerning specificity in an audit program, one fact remains: Audit standards for fieldwork must be adhered to; and that adherence must be documented, whether in the audit program or elsewhere in the working papers. When an auditor conducts fieldwork himself, however, or if work is performed by other auditors under his general supervision, he will most likely prepare and refer to the audit *program,* not the audit *guide.*

Audit Guides

What is an audit guide, and how does it differ from an audit program? Several of my colleagues responded to this question by saying that a guide is general, whereas a program is specific. By this means of distinction, some programs (such as Sawyer describes, for example) could almost as easily be called guides as programs. Furthermore, nothing any more helpful in making such a distinction was found in scanning the literature of auditing.

The most common use of the term "audit guide," however, seems to be in reference to situations wherein one auditor or agency must rely on fieldwork done by another auditor not under his or her direct control. Such is the case, for example, when federal agencies contract with CPA's or state or local governmental auditors for performance of a segment of a larger audit or for the audit of a grant at a particular location. One might also use the term "guide" to describe general instructions furnished to its own field offices by the central headquarters of a large audit organization.

In this context, audit guides should contain background material about the program or other audit subject, an explanation of the audit's objectives, stated expectations as to required reporting, and audit programs applicable to the audit subject of concern. [See, for example, *Suggested Guidelines for the Structure and Content of Audit Guides Prepared by Federal Agencies for Use by CPA's* (New York: American Institute of Certified Public Accountants, 1972) and Frederic A. Heim, Jr., "Integrating the GAO Audit Standards into Audit Guides," in *The Internal Auditor,* 31, No. 2 (March/April, 1974), pp. 79-82.] Programs contained within guides should give recognition to extant, generally accepted audit standards and auditor professionalism. There should be no need to provide detailed verification instructions regarding areas where the performing auditor's professional judgment should carry him through. At the same time, however, guides that require an auditor to venture into examinations that he may view as lying outside the domain of generally accepted auditing standards should contain more explicit instructions and verification procedures. The same may be said of examinations into audit subject matter about which the performing auditor may be dubious as to the existence of generally accepted evaluation criteria. Elaboration of this theme, of course, is outside the scope of this discussion.

Conclusion

Audit *programs* are the basic means by which an auditor obtains, and documents the obtainment of, sufficient competent evidential matter for the expression of an informed opinion. Audit guides, on the other hand, are more general and are the means by which a primary auditor or agency communicates general guidelines and instructions to *other* auditors who will perform work in the field. Audit guides may include audit programs, however, and those programs may be general or specific, depending largely upon the nature of the audit subject.

The Audit Survey . . . What and How

Allan L. Reynolds, CIA, CPA

The Internal Auditor July/Aug. 1975

The audit survey consists of those activities necessary to accumulate and to analyze information essential for establishing the scope and objectives of the audit and for preparing an efficient audit program to meet these objectives. More simply, the survey is a determination of what and how to audit.

There are a number of possible ways to structure the survey effort. Probably, none is clearly superior; but it is important that the process be disciplined. To be avoided is the rote gathering of data for the files without clear decisions as to expected analyses and identification of matters requiring conclusions.

Time should be spent in thinking through the survey's objectives before starting. A survey guide should be developed. The degree of formality or informality of this guide depends on the complexity of the undertaking and the skill and experience of those who will assist in the survey.

Supervisory Personnel Should Participate

It is also highly desirable for supervisory personnel to actively participate in the survey. Their firsthand participation and contribution to the decision process regarding scope, objectives, and time budgets will produce material savings. It will also help avoid intensive supervisory efforts which sometimes occur later when it is found that the audit has gone astray.

The approach to a survey may be

studied in relation to its several purposes:

- To obtain mission orientation
- To determine mission implementation
- To identify areas of sensitivity or problems of consequence
- To set the scope and objectives of the audit
- To prepare the program for audit verification

The Orientation

Orientation consists of determining the mission assigned to an organizational unit or functional program, including its short- and long-term objectives. Also, to be determined are the resources invested in carrying out the mission, the criteria prescribed for measuring mission accomplishment, and the control mechanisms: lines of authority, reporting requirements, etc., established to monitor mission performance, policy and procedural conformance, and financial accountability. While much of this information will tend to be available in documented form, discussions should be held with key management officials to confirm currency and pertinence. These discussions, coupled with firsthand observation of activities, add a sense of comprehension and reality to the orientation.

Review Internal Control System

The analysis of mission implementation involves a review of the activity's internal control system, including its plan of organization, policies and procedures, accounting and historical records, standards of performance, and reports. Particular attention should be addressed to feedback and control actions as they relate to the organization's efforts to carry out its mission. Generally, the depth of this portion of the survey will be variable, starting with a top-layer cut and probing deeper into those features which are particularly important to controlling mission accomplishment or which show potential weaknesses. Discussions with key operating personnel, walk-throughs of test transactions, and firsthand observations of the operations are key methodologies to be coupled with the "paperwork" review.

Identification of areas of sensitivity or problems of consequence will be based on the results of the foregoing review coupled with prior audit experience. Discussions with managers of the entity under audit and managers who supervise or control operations interfacing with the entity under audit are also critical elements. The final decisions will also place heavy emphasis on materiality.

How to Establish Scope and Objectives

To establish the scope and objectives of the audit, there should be explicit determination of the functions, activities, and period to be included or excluded from the audit. These should be documented in a survey summary. This summary should include a specification of detailed audit objectives which, in turn, are translated into:

- A statement of procedures or methodology for accomplishing the objectives; i.e., the audit program
- Time estimates and staff capabilities needed to accomplish the audit (resources needed)

To summarize, the survey effort should be directed at the end product of an audit plan. It should be a substantive rather than mechanical effort, generally requiring tailor-made survey guides. Audit supervisory effort should be directed to this critical phase of the audit effort. Finally, a considerable portion of the effort should be spent in talking with operational and management personnel and observing the operations of the activity under review.

Audit Priorities

Daniel D. Frawley, CPA

The Internal Auditor July/Aug. 1973

Legislative Operational Auditing was established in Wisconsin in 1966 and finally started in 1969. The new statutory charge was:

> *". . . Review the performance and program accomplishments of the agency during the fiscal period for which the audit is being conducted to determine whether the agency carried out the policy of the Legislature and the Governor."*

While the terms Operational Audit or Managerial Audit are preferred over the term Performance Audit, it is believed that the most accepted definition of this type of audit covers: (1) performing a financial audit, (2) determining that the work was performed in the most economical way (which is referred to as efficiency) and (3) assuring the degree to which the intent of the legislature and the governor was carried out (normally called effectiveness).

In these audits, what should be done to review programs for efficiency and effectiveness? First, it is admitted that the staff does not have the manpower to check every program for efficiency and effectiveness. Thus, the initial planning step is to establish the areas to be covered. In setting priorities the following must be determined:

- What are the total resources used in the program?
- Does it appear that the program will grow?
- Does the nature of the program require management to select alternate methods of reaching their goals?
- What is the interest of the legislature in the program?
- What audits have been requested by the legislature or the governor?
- Are statutory requirements being met?

It is clear that adequate planning

time for an audit is essential if the auditor is to avoid total chaos and delay in field audit time. In planning an audit the auditor must learn as much as possible about the agency by reviewing the applicable statutes, its budget, its reports, the prior post audits that are available. The auditor should ascertain what program goals have been established and whether these goals are specific enough to provide a basis to audit against.

A complete audit program is prepared to serve as a guide for the fieldwork. Naturally, this program is not a bible. If fieldwork indicates that more hours must be spent in an area that seems more productive for substantial audit findings, work in other areas has to be delayed for a later audit or the original time allotted for the audit increased. This obviously results in a changed audit program for later scheduled audits.

The total resources being used in the program combined with the auditor's best judgment as to whether the program is going to be an expanding one or is being phased out, are perhaps the most basic considerations given to allotting audit hours. These factors – combined with past conclusions on the effectiveness and efficiency of the agency's operation — basically determine the number of audit hours to be allotted and where the audit will fall into the priority schedule.

Naturally, time allowances for statutory audits and audits ordered by the governor or legislature will also reset the basic audit schedule.

Many agencies, of varying size, are easy to audit. These are primarily regulatory agencies of long standing in which a long history of statutory law, court decisions and Attorney General opinions has left the agency little room for options or administrative alternatives. Frequently these agencies – at least in Wisconsin – have advisory boards composed of most groups affected by their actions, i.e., The Public, Labor and Management. The recommendations of these advisory boards are usually given priority in the legislature. Therefore, the auditor can or need do little in aiding them to obtain new or needed legislation.

Other agencies are an entirely different ball game. They are new; they are controversial; their administrators may be of unknown quality; their staff may be new and untrained; most importantly of all, they may have options by the dozens all through their programs as to which course to pursue. A major audit obligation is to give data to the agency management, the governor and the legislature; so they can make effective selections from the various alternatives.

The auditor should not second guess the agency's decisions based on the facts available *a year or two after* the agency made a decision. The auditor is charged with the duty of determining whether or not the agency considered the options available to it to meet its goals with the facts available at the time of the original decision.

The Wisconsin field audit approach differs somewhat from that of the GAO. In Wisconsin, the auditor is charged with the full responsibility of financial audit and he uses this as his entry tool to operational audit rather than the GAO-type investigation.

This audit approach in government varies in some respects from that of the corporate internal auditor who has a definite charge and, to some extent, can leave financial audit to his corporation's CPA firm.

No form of audit can be as interesting and challenging as state audit, especially when the audit staff is innovative and able .

State audit groups must gain the full support of the AICPA and state CPA societies. More importantly, they must gain the support of the management of many firms with capable internal audit staffs and combine this support with the power of The Institute of Internal Auditors and the Cadmus Foundation.

When this has been attained, audit will have truly arrived at its goal: assisting management in achieving data to properly determine the priorities facing it.

At that time, government will be able to give the public the services it insists on – at the minimum cost.

Approaches to Synergetic Auditing

Ben F. Robinson, CIA

The Internal Auditor July/Aug. 1974

In the Office of Audit, U.S. Department of Agriculture, we have an affirmative action program directed toward minimizing the overlapping and duplication of work which has too often been a way of life for Federal audit staffs.

We have, for a number of years, had a policy which calls for fostering, and relying on – to the maximum extent possible as determined by periodic testing by our staff – the audits of USDA programs as performed by state, county or city audit staffs and by public accounting firms employed by those governmental jurisdictions.

Why We Rely on Other Audits

We were influenced in the establishment of this policy by the recognition that it is the primary responsibility of the state and local governments to effectively manage these programs; that an inherent part of management is the internal control function; and that audit is a key element of internal control. However, we also had a much more selfish motive dictated by the tremendous demands being placed upon us.

With a Food Stamp Program in practically every county and major city in the United States involving problems of accountability for cash and coupons amounting to over $4 billion annually; with a School Lunch Program in almost every school in the country expending over $1.5 billion of Federal funds each year, plus that much and more from matching funds within the

States; with a food distribution program of nationwide proportions; and with a cooperative meat and poultry inspection program attempting to assure that every bite of meat eaten in the U.S.A. is wholesome, it was impossible to foresee the Office of Audit providing all the necessary audit coverage.

We have taken many steps in moving toward the objectives envisioned in our policy.

Mutual Trust and Respect Vital

Recognizing that mutual respect and trust are vital to such an effort, we asked each of our Regional Directors to personally contact the likely (for coverage of USDA programs) audit staffs in their respective geographic areas. In these meetings they explained our organization, objectives and operating style. They identified, for the first time, what state audit groups were, and were not, doing in the way of reviews of USDA programs. Finally, they discussed ways whereby we could be of assistance to the states' expanded efforts in auditing USDA programs.

At the same time we encouraged state and local auditors to visit our Regional Offices to get acquainted with our managers and their staffs and to learn more about how we function – our recruiting, training, programming, scheduling and audit performance. The results of those initial contacts, plus several since, have been very encouraging. Our plan has been to continue to work with all of the state staffs but to give priority, naturally, to those who expressed eagerness to cooperate.

Audit Guides: A Basic Need

Early in these efforts we realized that basic to communicating audit needs are audit guides (or programs). So we prepared and distributed to the state audit staffs which might be concerned, such guides for each of our four major operating programs. These guides are an adaptation of those we use in our own audits. They set forth the standards and coverage we expect in the fiscal and compliance areas if we are to rely upon the work of another audit staff. As experience is gained, we plan to expand these guides to include tests of program efficiency and effectiveness.

Barriers Removed

As a corollary effort to the contacts being made by our regional managers, a series of seminars was held in Dallas, San Francisco, Atlanta, and New York City. Operating and audit officials were represented from both the Federal and state sides. These meetings were very helpful in getting out unforeseen problems for resolutions. But, more importantly, they went a long way in removing mythical barriers and in creating an atmosphere of friendly purposeful cooperation.

During the past two years we have assisted state auditors in preparing plans of audit which, when fully carried out, would reduce our coverage to the very minimum. We have helped state audit staffs to adapt our suggested guides to their particular operating constraints. We have assisted in designing pro-forma work papers, and we have provided background information on USDA programs and on past audits. But our biggest contribution to this cooperative effort has been in training.

In this training we explain the purposes and goals of the USDA program(s), the audit objectives related to the program goals, and the specific steps to accomplish the audit objectives. Seminars and workshops ranging from one to three days are used, as well as on-the-job training.

As an example, in one Midwestern state we joined with the audit staff of another Federal agency in a training session for 12 auditors responsible for audits of the Child Nutrition Programs. The training sessions consisted of 3½ days covering audit theory and practices, as well as program background. Later these 12 state auditors joined our auditors for about six weeks of on-the-job training.

ADP Audit Procedures Prove Helpful

More and more, state and local staffs are finding our ADP audit procedures to be beneficial. In a recent instance the Chief Auditor of a state department, along with selected members of his staff, came to our Washington office with an ADP problem which we were able to solve jointly. They brought along the magnetic tape recordings of one of the USDA programs in their state. We were able to demonstrate first-hand how we use an ADP packaged program to select samples which have the greatest likelihood of leading auditors to the problem areas. Since many states, cities and counties are using ADP to process data on USDA programs, we see this as an excellent area for future cooperative efforts with our state and local counterparts.

Other Helpful Forces at Work

Before concluding, I must point out that although we have been working at these cooperative relationships for several years – and achieving success – there have been other helpful forces at work.

The issuance of *"Standards for Audit of Governmental Organizations, Programs, Activities and Functions,"* by the General Accounting Office in 1972, as well as the recent supportive policies of the Office of Financial Management, General Services Administration, have done much to awaken management at all levels to the need for audits meeting "generally accepted standards."

Significant also are the Intergovernmental Audit Forums (National and Regional) composed of representatives of local, state and Federal audit staffs, who are meeting regularly, discovering their counterparts to be human beings after all, and jointly seeking solutions to obstacles to synergetic auditing.

Computer Auditing: A Basic Book

Robert V. Graham, CIA

The Internal Auditor Sept./Oct. 1974

Computer auditing is an integral and essential part of an audit of any organization with automated systems. It should not be classified as a separate or special audit but should be incorporated into the overall scope of the regular audit.

This philosophy is subscribed to by the Office of State Auditor and is mentioned here to set the tone for this discussion. The advancement of computer technology in recent years has made some form of automation available to virtually every governmental entity at all levels. The day has long passed where an auditor can function effectively without some knowledge of data processing.

This is not to say that all auditors must be computer auditors. To the contrary, every audit staff must have computer audit capability available to it. The auditing profession generally recognizes the need for a group or team of specialists to assist in the more technical aspects of computer auditing. However, this does not let the regular auditor off the hook. He must continue to upgrade his skills and capability in this area to handle the more routine areas of computer auditing. This, of course, will allow the specialist to concentrate on more advanced auditing.

Training for Computer Auditing

Computer audit training takes on two distinct features: first, the training necessary for the regular auditor with little or no experience in data processing; second the training necessary to keep a computer audit specialist abreast of the computer industry and advanced audit techniques.

The goal of this training program is to put more and more dependence on audit teams to conduct audits of computer installations and to evaluate internal control of automated systems. Auditors must be able to study and evaluate internal control of any system, manual or automated, if any audit program is to be successful. Further, this frees up the computer auditor for in-depth auditing such as file interrogation, testing, simulation and identifying exception situations for further review by audit teams.

Training is obviously the key to this effort. The auditors must be versed in data processing concepts, controls, terminology, security, etc. Most of this training can be provided by the computer auditors, but should include a mix of in-house, on-the-job and external training.

Types of Audits

To facilitate the training program and the direction of computer auditing in the Office of State Auditor, we have identified two specific types of audits: an installation audit and a systems audit. Let me explain.

An installation audit involves only the data processing organization. The scope is narrowly defined to include only those activities occurring within the computer center and does not attempt to trace them through other departments.

General areas reviewed in this form of audit are:

1. Organization
   a. Location of EDP department
   b. Separation of duties
   c. Use of resources
   d. Setting priorities
   e. Personnel
2. Security
   a. Access
   b. Fire protection and suppression
   c. Files
   d. Disaster plan
   e. Emergency procedures
   f. Backup
   g. Insurance
3. Controls
   a. Input
   b. Processing
   c. Output
4. Documentation
   a. Systems
   b. Program
   c. Operator

Initially, heavy emphasis was placed on installation audits because of the need for basic security and control measures. As installations improve in these areas, the audit emphasis shifts to a more data oriented philosophy.

A general audit of an automated system consists of at least these areas:

1. Documentation
   a. Standards
   b. Systems
   c. Program
   d. Operator
2. Organization
   a. Separation of duties
   b. Use of resources
   c. Personnel
3. Input
   a. Authorization
   b. Controls
4. Processing
   a. Edits
   b. Correction routines
   c. Reentry
5. Output
   a. Controls
   b. Distribution
6. Software package
   a. File interrogation
   b. Confirmations
   c. Simulation

You will note that the areas reviewed are generally the same in both types of audits except for two things: the systems audit transcends departments and it usually includes some file interrogation.

Audit Software

The most common method now used for reviewing data files is an audit software package. Many firms have developed their own software packages and are marketing them to some extent. They are available to the public, although in most cases, much control over their use is maintained by the firm that developed it.

Generally, an audit software package consists of a series of generalized programs which allow the user to select, compute, compare, sort and otherwise manipulate data to produce an output that can be used to facilitate the audit process. Most software can also print confirmations at the auditor's discretion.

Some audit groups are still spending the time necessary to develop their own specialized audit programs. This is usually not cost effective except for specific recurring applications.

The use of an audit software package should be an extension of the audit process. The study and evaluation of internal control should determine the need for review of the data files.

Playing Computer Catch-Up

Computer auditing is a relatively new technique. Those who disagree that it is a technique must certainly agree it is a new dimension in auditing. Over the past twenty years, computers and automated processes have gradually replaced traditional manual systems. During this period, the auditor grew more and more detached from the actual processing of data. Thus, we find audit programs which are at least four to five years behind the computer industry. We are not keeping up, although we are catching up.

On the bright side, there has been an extensive effort the past few years to develop computer audit capabilities on audit staffs and even to develop computer audit specialists. There are several professional organizations available to computer auditors and some excellent publications dealing with the subject. We can no longer ignore what has existed for many years.

The approach outlined in this article is a temporary one. It stems largely from the lack of planning as installations were built and developed over the years. As planning begins to be recognized as an essential part of any process, we can expect the necessity of an installation audit to decrease and the importance of the data oriented or systems audit to take its rightful place in the total audit process.

Statistical Sampling and the Computer

William Wilkerson, CIA

The Internal Auditor December 1976

When auditors learn to use a generalized computer audit system, many of them think they will no longer need to deal with statistical sampling (hereafter referred to as sampling) since the computer works so rapidly that auditing operations can be carried out 100%. There is an element of truth to this feeling because some actions that were only practicable on a sampling basis can now be done for the entire population.

Finding Elusive Items

An example of this kind of action is the search for apparent duplicate submission of bills for payment. Formerly, to find even possible examples of these duplicate payments required weeks of sampling effort. After learning to use a computer audit system, the auditor can isolate all examples of possible duplicate payments in a day or so. So here is a case where the computer apparently does a job which previously required a sampling approach.

However, the auditor may be inundated with a computer listing containing hundreds — or even thousands — of examples of possible duplicate payments. The auditor must turn to sampling to determine how many of the possible duplicate payments are actually duplicates and what their estimated value is in the population of possible duplicate payments. In this case, the auditor has been able to use the computer to quickly perform an audit step which formerly was done by sampling, only to find another need for sampling.

This example shows how the computer can be used in an audit to find and concentrate, or stratify into a subpopulation, items which usually would be scattered throughout a population and which would have to be located by sampling. The stratification enables the auditor to develop efficient sampling plans for evaluating these subpopulations.

Replication of Processes

The auditor can also use the computer to replicate a process to be evaluated which formerly could be evaluated only by sampling. An example of this approach would be the reprocessing of all transactions for an accounting period to evaluate the posting of ledger accounts and to verify their balances.

Again, the auditor must examine a statistical sample of the transactions to determine that they are, in fact, supported. This example demonstrates a second major way in which the computer can do a job formerly requiring sampling, but one in which sampling is needed to verify the basic data.

Enhancement of Audit Quality

These two general computer audit approaches show how using the computer in place of a sample can result in a sample being needed to complete the job. Note that in both cases the quality and timeliness of audit information should be greatly enhanced over previous approaches. This illustrates the value of combining computer and sampling techniques in auditing.

Ubiquity of Need

An organization large enough to have an internal audit staff would, in all probability, use computers to generate transactions in sufficient numbers so that they could be effectively examined only by sampling and computer audit techniques. Any organization using computers for administrative purposes would, in all probability, have sufficient volume to require the application of sampling for internal auditing. The great increase in minicomputers means that most auditors, even those in small organizations, will have to evaluate large volumes of data in their work.

Conclusion

The need for applying sampling is intensified by the use of computer audit techniques. The combination of computer audit techniques and sampling enables the internal auditor to handle in an efficient and effective way the great masses of computerized data formerly regarded as making auditing more and more difficult.

The use of computer audit techniques may change the approach to sampling. Computer audit techniques may also increase the need for sampling, however. With the computer, the auditor can create situations where sampling is advantageous. These situations will provide more and better information for management — information previously not obtainable in many cases.

Quality Control — Audit and Report

Franklin C. Pinkelman, CPA

The Internal Auditor July/Aug. 1975

Recently, widespread attention has been focused on the dynamic changes in governmental auditing in the past few years. Attention has, in the main, been concentrated on two subject areas: (1) Standards of audit practice in the audit and the audit organization was the subject of a study of the GAO, resulting in the promulgation of *Standards for Audit of Governmental Organizations, Programs, Activities and Functions* by the comptroller general of the United States. At the same time and partially as a result of the same publication, there has been an intense interest in (2) changing the purpose of the audit, directing our attention to the need for audits which review the efficiency of operations and effectiveness of governmental programs. There is little question in my mind that these efforts were well directed and will continue to bear fruit.

I suggest, however, that there is a need to renew our interest in another item of concern important to the success of governmental audit efforts. Recent changes demand another look at quality control of audit activities and the reporting process. I believe that expansion, changing direction, or changing conditions require more, not less control.

Some would argue just the opposite. They make the point that control often tends to stifle innovations and creative development. I suggest that we must take that risk if we are to continue to provide service and information with a high degree of credibility.

Quality control in the auditing and reporting processes should be a prime bulwark in assuring our clients that we obtain sufficient data to make sound analyses, we are fair in our conclusions and recommendations, and we are accurate in our reporting.

Quality Control Anchored to Guidelines

Quality control, as it applies to audit activities, relates to the conducting of the actual examination as well as to any reports issued as a result of the examination. As far as the audit is concerned, control of fieldwork should be anchored to the audit guidelines. We have the responsibility for a full-fledged financial audit as well as a performance audit. Audit guidelines specifically tailored to the individual audit are prepared for each audit, updated, and reviewed at the completion of any audit assignment.

On-the-site supervisors are responsible to determine adherence to the guidelines except where adjustments are approved. Adjustments can be made when certain conditions prevail and when general departmental policy is followed. When conditions or procedures have materially changed at the agency being audited, the audit supervisor will review the new information with the audit manager; and together they will adjust as appropriate.

However, when deletions which are substantial and crucial to the fundamental financial examination are planned, these must be reviewed by someone at the executive level. Additions are often left to the discretion of the manager since these typically affect the audit time budget, and overages of time are expected to be justified.

The practice of using the audit guideline for audit-quality-control purposes is, of course, dependent on some other significant factors. It is important that guidelines be significantly more than simple checklists; it is even more important that the guideline in use be current and specific to the audit being conducted.

Guidelines for New Types of Audit

This brings forth the question as to guidelines for new jobs or for new types of auditing. In these cases, a short general guideline specific to the purposes of the audit is prepared. This short outline is then developed into a full guideline as facts and conditions become better known and as the audit progresses. These, then, are subject to review by someone above the field-supervisory level.

One other important factor relating to control through guidelines lies in the training of members of the audit organization. Each and every member of the organization must be committed to quality in the audit. This can only be accomplished if all are aware of the need for control; but, more importantly, members of the staff are not only expected to understand the guidelines but also are free to challenge them through a well-established process of review.

Work-Paper Review

It is the province of a well-designed work paper and audit review process to insure that the report reflects a sound audit. The process should include a detailed item-by-item-work-paper review by the site supervisor, a less detailed review of work papers by audit managers, and a technical review after the report has been submitted at the conclusion of the field operation. The supervisor's review should, in the main, be concerned with adherence to the guidelines and assurance that the auditor did not leave any loose ends.

This review results in the writing of the audit exception and the recommendations. The purpose of the audit manager's review of the work papers is at least twofold: (1) He conducts a less-detailed review of the work papers to satisfy himself about the audit, and (2) he reviews specific work papers to insure the quality of the individual item in the audit report.

When the audit is completed and when the pencil copy of the report is submitted to the report-review section, the work papers are turned over to the work-paper-review section. The work-paper-review section conducts a detailed technical review of the work papers, making judgment on form and content according to specific criteria. The total package is scored, and the supervisor and manager are called in for a discussion about the quality of the work papers. The same section conducts a review of the updated guidelines and discusses them with the audit manager.

Review of the Audit Report

The pencil copy of the report is reviewed by the report-review section. Here, we are concerned with accuracy in citation of laws, rules, or regulations; grammar and composition of the narrative; consistency with items dealt with in other reports; propriety of schedules and audit-item headings; accuracy in amounts, percentages, footings, etc.; completeness in the description of the agency and the audit scope; and general presentation of the report.

The first typed copy is then reviewed by the audit manager and the executive level. At this stage, we apply final judgment on the content of the report. Some changes may be made in presentation, but the principal focus is on the preparation of a report which is constructive rather than destructive. We also want to be sure that analyses warrant conclusions drawn and that recommendations are relevant and reasonable to problem conditions.

As cited, the processes provide what, we feel, is most necessary to quality control in the audit and the report. There are other things which contribute, however. Some of them are the audit conference with the agency; review of second drafts and final reports; and selection, training, and orientation of personnel.

Quality Control Essential

In the final analysis, it is my belief that quality control is one of the most important aspects of the audit process. We must not be satisfied with the status quo, especially when, as now, the audit environment is changing. Faith and credibility on the part of our clients are absolutely necessary to continued success.

Evaluating the Effectiveness of The Audit Operation

Daniel D. Frawley, CPA

The Internal Auditor Sept./Oct. 1973

How well would your audit agency look under the light of a good operational audit by an independent auditing team? Could you reply satisfactorily to the "why" of your operation? What is your objective and how effectively are you carrying it out? Do you have your goals clearly spelled out? Do you really have a planned audit program to accomplish your mission? Or is your program a hit and miss affair with brush fires being fought, requests for really non-productive audits always being honored and very little in productive operational audit being realized?

How competent is your staff? What training are you giving to increase its competency? Have you allotted enough time and resources in your budget to develop the staff and climate you need for real operational audit?

You certainly would be asked this final question as to your effectiveness by a second auditor – How many of your recommendations have been implemented?

It is possible that many of our audit agencies would not be covered with glory if an independent report were issued on their efficiency and effectiveness. Our own audit agencies might be well advised to take time for a long look at their own operations. If we know our own faults, we can take the necessary steps to eliminate or to substantially correct them. But have we taken the time for an objective look at ourselves?

We may have made such a strong commitment to quality audits of *other* agencies that our own operations may well have been overlooked. The shortage of manpower and money in many central audit agencies may have resulted in the postponement of their own planning, training and use of experts and consultants, as well as our failure to recruit the quality of individual we need for competent operational audit.

The time to start correcting the deficiencies in our own operations is yesterday and not after we have been audited by outsiders.

I propose that we start with examining our own organizational structure. Is it fundamentally sound? Are responsibilities clearly defined and authority given to meet duties? Are provisions incorporated into the system for proper communications both up and down? Have we done our entire job in recruiting new people? Are we getting people with the proper mix of education and experience to do the job required? What training are we offering the new staff man? What are we doing to change our older staff into competent operational auditors?

We can continue to examine or audit our own operation in many fashions. What audit priorities have we established? Do we consider audit planning the mere drafting of an individual audit program or, rather, do we look at an overall concept of state audit? Pure financial audit may be required and needed in many areas. But what is our view of "big picture" operational audit?

Have we established the necessary priorities to enable us to cover all major divisions of our state departments to obtain the maximum benefit of our audit hours? Or, are our priorities confused and our measurements shaky?

Have we incorporated the latest audit methods into our audits to save audit time? Have we programmed our audits to achieve maximum results with minimum time? These are fair questions which we may be called to answer some day.

Can we truly be called effective? What are our audit results? Some audit agencies attempt to show cost savings over audit costs in ranges from two-to-one or as high as ten-to-one. Is this really advisable? Some wonder if the provable dollar savings are really the reason for our existence. Perhaps the dark grey area of cost savings combined with radical or basic improvement in the audited agencies' management should be our major goal.

What is our relationship with our auditees? Would a second auditor conclude that there was a basically good relationship, mutually concerned with improvement in management, or that it was a strictly antagonistic or adversary role? We must remember that our goal is the improvement of state service both as to efficiency and economy. We do not exist just to second guess or criticize, or to write "good" audit reports.

We are paid from tax money and we want an independent audit or evaluation to conclude that our worth is more than our cost.

Hopefully we would, on independent judgment, be considered a good and useful management tool rather than just a passing management fancy.

What are your answers to the questions posed here?

Sufficiency of Audit Evidence in Differing Audit Environments

Edward P. Chait, CPA

The Internal Auditor August 1976

Both the AICPA and the GAO "yellow book" standards say that an auditor shall examine sufficient and competent evidence to form an audit conclusion.

The amount of evidence needed in a financial and compliance audit depends on the extent of internal accounting controls, materiality to the financial statements, and audit risk. Based on his understanding of the entity's records and internal accounting controls, the auditor will determine what documents to sample and what information to record in his working papers. All of these relate to measurement criteria contained in financial statements and to applicable laws and regulations with respect to compliance.

What similar determinations should be made in audits of economy and efficiency and program results — operational audits?

Measurement Criteria

To determine sufficiency of audit evidence in operational auditing, the auditor must first determine measurement criteria for efficiency, economy, and program results. An integral part of the operational audit is the definition of those measurement criteria that allow the auditor to form meaningful conclusions.

For example, in a financial audit the auditor may decide to substantiate accounts payable balances by examining invoices for all vendor balances over a certain dollar amount and only a small sample of the remaining balances.

In an operational audit, where the auditor might be interested in the efficiency and effectiveness with which purchases are made, the dollar amount of accounts payable is not significant.

The determination of sufficient evidence in an operational audit will depend to a great extent on the definition of the criteria to be measured.

In defining measurement criteria, the auditor must consider certain characteristics. The basic characteristics of measures of efficiency and economy generally are those associated with productivity — cost-per-unit, revenues-per-unit, etc.

The basic characteristics of measure-of-program effectiveness are (1) comparisons of costs and benefits before and after a program to determine the effect of the program and (2) comparison of productivity measures of similar organizations.

The amount and types of evidence examined to support these defined measurement criteria will, by their nature, vary from examination to examination. Such variations are not typically found in financial and compliance auditing performed under specific auditing standards.

Competence of Evidence Examined

It is important that measurement criteria and related evidence allow meaningful conclusions to be drawn. The evidence examined should be sufficient and competent enough to support the identified problems, causes, and recommendations.

For example, an auditor might note a case of decreased product output or service per man-hour. Based on his discussions with employees or his observation of employees — evidence — he may attribute the decreases to low employee morale caused by a low rate of pay and/or poor working conditions.

To be sure that the prudent man believes such a finding, the auditor should be certain that the sample of employees surveyed is representative of the organization. Also, the decreased output should bear a cause and effect relationship to specific differences in working conditions —pay rates not keeping pace with those of employees in similar positions of responsibility. Enough competent evidence should be examined so that the prudent man can draw meaningful conclusions.

Reporting Results of Evidence Examined

In financial and compliance audit reports, the auditor will generally refer to specific auditing standards as the scope of his examination. He will state an opinion about the entity or project being examined.

In an operational audit, the auditor may not form an opinion about the overall entity or project being examined except to state that, based on his study, he observed there were *x* number of instances in which the predefined criteria were not met. He will also make recommendations. The measurement criteria and the amount of evidence examined, fully discussed in the auditor's report, are matters of professional judgment. The reader must be fully informed about the extent of the audit, including the scope of the review, the findings and conclusions of the review, and the auditor's recommendations. If the measurement was properly made, conclusions and recommendations should be self-evident.

Conclusion

The traditional, financial statement benchmarks of sufficiency of audit evidence are similar to the benchmarks used in operational auditing. These benchmarks are simply used in a different environment — a different type of audit testing. Evidence supporting the conclusion must still be sufficient and competent. That is, the auditor must examine enough evidence to make conclusions and recommendations believable.

What Is Reliability

Dr. T. Arthur Smith

The Internal Auditor August 1976

When it comes to common usage, the English language can be deceptive. For example, take the word *reliability.*

Reliability can have several meanings to the auditor who depends on common usage. He relates *reliable* and *reliability.*

The first term is a general one that concerns itself with the question: Can I trust this evidence and/or its source? Depending upon the nature of the audit, the auditor may have to depend upon external or internal sources of evidence. The evidence itself might be obtained orally or from hard copy. Obviously, the auditor has to concern himself with both the dependability of the source and the validity of specific data.

In the consideration of manual controls, the auditor uses the term *reliable* as a subjective criterion to evaluate the success of the controls in capturing and cross-checking information. In considering automated controls, the auditor also pays attention to the possibility of data substitution and manipulation.

Statistical Validity

Reliability has an entirely different meaning. Rather than being synonymous with such words as good, factual, valid, or, perhaps, dependable, the term has a very precise meaning and is based on statistical validity.

Another term for reliability is *statistical confidence level.* Reliability is expressed as a percentage. The percentage expresses the degree of assurance that the results of a statistical sample are representative of the population being sampled. Another way of looking at the term is that reliability in audit evidence is not the converse of *wrong.* It is the converse of *risk.*

There are several operational problems associated with the reliability of audit evidence. One such problem relates to the competence displayed in the implementation of the statistical process itself. Bedingfield,[1] in his survey of the use of statistical sampling by CPA's, found that 23% of the respondents noted lack of adequate training as the major drawback to using statistical sampling in audits. He also found that 20% thought that sample selection was difficult enough to qualify as a drawback. Thirteen percent mentioned as another drawback the fact that their staffs had some difficulty in interpreting the results of a statistical sample. The Bedingfield article warrants the attention of all auditors not contemplating retirement in the near future.

Morris's observation[2] that the auditor must be willing to spend time learning how to apply statistics is a particularly good observation.

Statistics Can Be Deceptive

Statistics may be deceptive to the auditor — and sometimes to the statistician. Once assumptions are made regarding the population being examined, the statistical analysis can proceed with great mathematical rigor. The deceptiveness arises from the fact that, during the course of data collection and analysis, the auditor may uncover information that indicates the assumptions are invalid. Or even worse, such information, although there, may not be uncovered. There is a tendency, however, to fit observed data to the selected statistical technique since one is so engrossed in the mechanics of the procedure that implications affecting the assumptions are overlooked.

One example of this can be drawn from regression analysis, a relatively simple technique. The statistical confidence level can be precisely determined in regression analysis only to the extent that the conclusions drawn are within the range of the data. However, there is a tendency, when a projection is needed, to extend the projection beyond the limits of the observed data. This may be a valid procedure under some circumstances. But the auditor must realize that the statistical confidence level for the extension is not the same as the confidence level within the limits of the observed data.

[1]Bedingfield, James P., "The Current State of Statistical Sampling and Auditing," *Journal of Accountancy,* December 1975.

[2]Morris, Norman, "Statistical Sampling in Retrospect," *The Internal Auditor,* January/February 1976.

Audit Evidence and Relevance

Dr. Herbert A. O'Keefe, Jr.

The Internal Auditor August 1976

The effectiveness of an audit is directly related to the acceptability of the audit opinion or the degree of implementation of the audit recommendation. One of the key factors to gaining this necessary acceptance is the sufficiency and competency of the supporting evidence. In auditing, competency implies both validity and relevance.

The subject of the relevance of audit evidence is therefore a legitimate area of inquiry for anyone who wishes to fully understand the audit process.

Relevant audit evidence is any information that reduces uncertainty about the acceptability of an assertion made by the entity under audit. The assertion can be explicit or implicit, financial or operational. However, it must be an assertion that is subject to audit.

In order for an assertion to be subject to audit, relevant evidence must be available to provide for acceptance or rejection of the assertion. The failure to recognize this audit limitation is a serious weakness in any audit.

Identify Auditable Assertions

Accordingly, one of the first steps in the audit is the identification of the auditable assertions. There are times when financial and operational assertions are made in the aggregate. In order to audit these aggregate assertions, the auditor must break them down into auditable assertions.

For example, in a financial audit a major balance sheet assertion may be stated as follows: Machinery - $25,000. In the aggregate this assertion is not subject to audit. However, the assertion can be broken down into the following auditable assertions: (1) a model OAG fabricating machine, serial number 6791, is in existence, (2) the entity owned the machine at the balance sheet date, and (3) the machine had an original cost of $25,000.

Physically examining the machine is relevant to the assertion that the machine is in existence. But it is not relevant to the other two assertions presented.

Examining the purchase contract should provide evidence relevant to the assertion that the machine cost $25,000. But it will not provide evidence relevant to the first assertion. The purchase contract may provide evidence that, at the time of the contract, the entity acquired ownership of the machine. But this evidence would not be the only relevant evidence needed to accept assertion two.

As a result, it is suggested that all entity assertions must be presented in auditable form so that the relevancy of the purported evidence can be adequately evaluated. If this is not done, it is possible that critical assertions will be accepted or rejected without the necessary relevant evidence being presented.

Degree of Relevance

The degree of relevance inherent in a specific piece of evidence is also an important audit consideration. In the preceding assertion concerning the existence of the fabricating machine, the physical evidence provided by examining the machine was of a higher degree of relevance than provided by the examination of an agreement with a contractor showing the machine out on lease or the certification of the existence of the machine by an independent third party.

Each of these pieces of evidence is relevant to the assertion, but some are more relevant than others. Consequently, the auditor is continually challenged to acquire the evidence that is most relevant to the assertion under examination.

The availability of relevant audit evidence and the cost of acquiring this evidence are also critical audit considerations. In order to develop appropriate strategy for gathering audit evidence, the trade-off between the additional cost of gathering the evidence and the benefit of that evidence to the audit objectives must be evaluated.

In this evaluation, the risks associated with the trade-offs should be a major input into the decision process. This evaluation is extremely sensitive to the value inputs provided by the auditor's professional judgment. The auditor must be careful not to yield completely to this judgment.

Auditing Is an Art

In considering the importance of relevance to the evidence-gathering process, it should be remembered that auditing is an art — an art that uses the scientific approach, but nonetheless an art. This art is further complicated because it is practiced in conjunction with other arts: accounting, operational management, policy execution.

Because auditing is an art, rarely will audit evidence provide full knowledge about the acceptability of an assertion. Acceptance or rejection of the assertion will normally be made on the basis of the preponderance of evidence.

In conclusion, judgment on audit evidence is tempered by the availability of relevant evidence, the cost of gathering this evidence, and the degree of relevance of the evidence to the assertion under examination.

At this point one should ask: Was this article relevant?

Permanent File Material for Internal Auditors

Grady Fullerton, CPA

The Internal Auditor Mar./April 1973

The internal auditor in local government has a unique opportunity to adopt many of the techniques that have proven to be so effective by independent public accounting firms. One of these techniques is to develop a permanent file. The following is a description of the material that could go into such a file and that should be kept current during the course of the year.

Photocopy of Enabling Legislation

Since any unit of government is created by the constitution or the state legislature, a complete file of the enabling legislation should be readily available. Such information is often not easy to locate. This file would include a copy of the applicable sections of the state constitution, state statutes, leading cases, attorney general opinions, and local government attorney's opinions. Also included would be copies of resolutions, ordinances or orders of the local government.

It is well to remember that a unit of local government is a "municipal" corporation (a generic term) rather than a "private" corporation. There are major philosophical differences between the two. It is well settled that a "municipal" corporation can do only those things that are specifically enumerated. The implied powers are strictly limited. This pertains not only to the unit of local government but also to elected or appointed officials.

What might well be an "ordinary and necessary business expense or reasonable in amount" for a private corporation could well be an illegal expenditure for a municipal corporation.

Bylaws

This section would apply primarily to units of local government that operate as enterprises; i.e., electric utilities, water utilities, airports, hospital districts, port authorities, etc. The section would have information about qualification of directors, requirements to call special meetings, provisions for board committees, officers (number and titles), duties of officers, accounting and auditing requirements, and other matters affecting accounting or auditing.

Bond Indentures and Long-term Debt Provisions

Units of government in the enterprise field sometimes issue revenue bonds, and the bond indentures often have rather complicated provisions for the creation of separate funds for the benefit and protection of the bond holder. Often there are specific requirements for setting up special bank accounts for each fund and transferring cash between funds each month.

The agreement with the paying agent will contain information as to the time the semiannual payments are to be sent to the paying agent, cash or deposit with the paying agent, return of paid bonds and coupons, return of cash for bonds and coupons not presented, and compensation to be paid to the paying agent.

Each bond indenture, including general obligation bonds, will include the following information: Title of indebtedness; principal amount; denomination of bonds; date of issue; maturity dates and terms; interest rates and terms; supplemental interest coupons, if any; redemption privileges; sinking fund requirement, if any; and most important of all, the "purpose clause" for which the proceeds of the bond issue may be spent.

Excerpts of Minutes

It is typical of local government to require much more documentation in the form of official minutes of meetings of commissioners, city council, and board of managers than is often found in private corporations. Prior approval of all contracts, including employee contracts, and even a detailed list of claims (vouchers) paid are included in the minutes of some units.

Organizational and Operational Charts

This section should include a general organizational chart of the unit or officer being audited. It is desirable to include a space diagram of the office layout and names of persons assigned to the various desks. Also included could be an accounting department organization chart; a chart of the flow of the service operations; and relationships with other local government offices.

Detailed Writeup of the Accounting System

This section would include an index of material pertaining to internal control; an organization of the internal control system to be used in the unit; a schedule of the annual review of the various phases of accounting procedures in internal control; a copy of the accounting manual, if any; a chart of accounts; a description of principal accounting records and forms; and memoranda on procedures and internal control.

Copies of Letters or Informal Comments on Internal Control

Included in this section would be a review of pertinent information from previous annual audit reports; a review of critical information coming from the annual service report sometimes issued by the unit; a review of any internal publications and special rules and regulations affecting the office; a list of officers and employees authorized to sign or approve vouchers, invoices, payrolls, writeoffs of receivables for service, credit memoranda, and persons authorized to enter safety deposit boxes.

Audit Tests Schedule

This is unique because it is not uncommon in units of local government for some internal work to be performed on a 100 per cent basis periodically, such as monthly. The schedule should show precisely who did the work, when, and the period of time that was covered in the examination. This would be particularly applicable in cash receipts, surprise examination of ready cash, reconciliation of bank accounts, purchases, payrolls, sales and services, and any receivable confirmations. This would also include a schedule of confirmation of traffic tickets paid in the past. Done on a statistical sampling test basis, this can give the auditor a feeling as to whether or not the collected cash has all been deposited.

An Index to Continuing Computations, Historical Analysis of Accounts

This would include analysis of plant property and equipment, an analysis of revenue by category by years, an analysis of expenditures by type of accounts by years, an analysis of the number of units of service rendered annually by years.

Important Newspaper Articles

This would include newspaper accounts or articles that have a direct bearing on the activities of the particular unit of government. This is a unique source of information about the activities of a particular office, such as the sheriff using a helicopter for traffic control or in connection with disaster relief.

Transfer List

This would include a complete list of items taken from the permanent file and stored in the inactive file.

It should be clear that the audit program, the internal control questionnaires or questionnaires about the use of data processing equipment are to be included in the permanent file. These are filed with the audit program file.

Operational Audits of Counties in Michigan

James J. Bolthouse, CPA

The Internal Auditor Sept./Oct. 1974

The Michigan Department of Treasury has, through the years, performed numerous financial and compliance audits of local governments. In virtually every audit, the Department felt that something more was both needed and desired.

A review of these audit reports will show that an occasional comment was directed at improving the efficiency or effectiveness of a particular program or activity. These comments were mainly the result of the auditors' knowledge of practices in other counties. rather than as a result of audit procedures directed toward improving efficiency or effectiveness.

When the U. S. General Accounting Office issued recommended governmental audit standards in 1972, the temptation was great to include in our scope, reference to the new standards. However, it doesn't take an expert in semantics to interpret the second general standard directed at the professional competence of the auditors who must "possess adequate ultimate proficiency for the tasks required." Our adoption of the audit standards would require an assessment of our present proficiency and a determination of what new skills were needed.

Our central office staff researched available materials on performance auditing, attended conferences on the subject and discussed the topic, but still felt the need to get some "hands-on" experience.

We were fortunate, indeed, to organize a joint audit team with the Detroit office of the U. S. General Accounting Office to actually perform efficiency-effectiveness audits of four selected county programs. Obviously, not everyone can receive "on the job training," but possibly our lessons learned from this experience will be of benefit to others.

Planning the Audit

The work program is a vital part of the financial audit and even more so in efficiency-effectiveness audits. It is very tempting to audit all phases and operations of a program or activity, but a well developed work program will center on those areas where the promise of improvement is greatest. It follows that the survey portion of the audit is highly critical to the ultimate success or failure of the audit. In addition to gathering basic information about the program, such as statutory objectives, effectiveness measures developed by trade associations or recognized national groups, organization patterns, etc., the survey should conclude whether or not a detailed audit should be performed and if so, where.

Timing the Audit

Where possible, performance type audits should be conducted as extensions of the traditional financial audit. Many audit workpapers can be expanded to document the procedures which were applied. For example, the logical time to examine the alternatives available to management for a capital outlay program is when the actual expenditure is being tested or vouched.

From our experience to date (which is acknowledged to be limited to two program audits), it appears that the effectiveness-efficiency portions of the audit consume two or three times as much audit time as the traditional financial compliance audit. It cannot be emphasized too much that the survey discussed above concludes whether or not a detailed audit is necessary. Audit efforts are a part of the overall system of internal control and like any other internal control measure, the benefits received should be measured against the costs incurred.

Delivering the Report

One of the most refreshing aspects of the entire audit is the conference with management over the preliminary report. Our reports are made to elected county officials whose political careers can be upset by a carelessly phrased audit comment. Auditors speak a language called "auditese" which, as you may suspect, is only understood by auditors. Be responsive to suggestions for changes in words and phrases which make the report more understandable. Be especially responsive to the thoughts of responsible management, who may reach a different conclusion from the same set of facts, and include them in the report.

Those who audit the public sector of our economy know the problems associated with exposure of preliminary audit comments by the news media. We know of no foolproof way to insure that preliminary comments won't be misconstrued. Our advice is to work with the news media by giving them the status of the audit in a timely manner. Point out the purpose of the preliminary draft and that it is subject to major revision. Promise to release the final official report promptly and assure them that the report will include the position of management in addition to the auditors. When it has been explained in these terms, we have had excellent media cooperation and have found that the media can be the single strongest force in the acceptance and ultimate adoption of our recommendations. And that is precisely what we're after, isn't it?

The State of Michigan performs audits of county government under legislation enacted in 1919 and supervises auditing performed by independent accountants for cities, villages and townships under legislation enacted in 1968.

8

cooperation with public accountants

Auditing in state and local governments has been the province of the public accountants for many years because the basic need was for an accountant to examine and to certify financial statements to be used for issuing bonds. Also, some governments were required by state law to have their statements audited periodically by independent public accountants. However, many governments employed auditors who performed both fiscal pre- and postaudits. The state of New York has had an internal audit operation of this type for over 100 years.

When operational internal auditing became better known during the 1940's, some progressive governments became interested. The federal government started operational audits during the late 1940's and early 1950's. State governments followed a few years later. The more than eighty thousand local governments comprise the last holdout. Here, too, we see progress. Of 650 auditors who responded to a recent survey of local government auditing, 362 reported that they perform operational (performance) audits, usually in concert with fiscal or compliance postaudits.

Governments have seen in the internal audit operation a benefit directly associated with the requirements for outside audits. Through a cooperative arrangement, independent public accountants were seen as extensions of the internal audit efforts of the government or vice versa. The outside auditor was asked to use the internal auditor to the greatest degree possible so as to keep fees at a minimum. And, after testing, the examination of internal controls routinely performed by the internal auditor could serve the external audit as well. Thus, a relationship has developed in which the two audit staffs combine to perform an effective financial/compliance audit.

With the advent of the operational audit, some governments tended to use independent public accountants to perform this type of work as well. Illinois, Colorado, and North Dakota were quite active in this area. Following a traumatic exposure of malfeasance, the requirement for the engagement of outside auditors became statutory in Illinois. The other two states engaged such services on a convenience basis, thereby obtaining the use of a qualified multidisciplined staff without keeping a large staff on the state payroll.

Two articles in this chapter describe the CPA relationship in Illinois and North Dakota. David B. Thomas, the first auditor general of Illinois, describes his use of a corps of 45 public accounting firms to conduct state audits. Chester E. Nelson, Jr., legislative budget analyst and auditor for the North Dakota Legislature, relates his state's experiences with the use of private accounting firms.

When and how to rotate the external auditing firm is always a problem. How it was resolved in Wichita, Kansas, is told by Lyle D. Botkin, city comptroller. Finally, Hugh Dorrian, city auditor of Columbus, Ohio, describes the methods used by his office for engaging CPA firms to perform financial postaudits.

The Use of Independent Public Accountants for State Audits

David B. Thomas, CPA

The Internal Auditor Nov./Dec. 1973

The Illinois Auditing Act requires that all state agencies, including universities, be audited at least every two years. This entails approximately 125 audit assignments each year. To perform these audits, the Auditor General relies almost entirely on independent public accounting firms. He uses approximately 50 firms, most of which have participated in the program for more than ten years and have State of Illinois auditing experience at all staff levels.

Each year the audit cycle begins with the decision on the average hourly rates to be paid for the next year's audits. The Auditor General then:

- Decides what audit assignments to offer each firm. Usually, he adheres to a five-audit rotation policy. For a new assignment he considers a firm's past performance; size and complexity of the audit in relation to availability of audit and management services staff; experience in similar audits; and geographic location of the assignment.
- Prepares an assignment file for each audit, containing prior audit reports, the booklet, "Instructions for Post-Audits of Illinois State Agencies," and other relevant materials.
- Asks if the firm will accept the established average rates. If so, he gives them the assignment files for the audits being offered and asks that they make a survey of each assignment. At this initial meeting he also gives special instructions, discusses audit objectives, and makes known his desire for them to suggest areas warranting special concern in their assignments (i.e, areas of efficiency, economy, and program results, etc.).
- Sends a letter of introduction to the state agency saying that

they can expect "X" firm to make an initial audit survey.

- Negotiates the estimated hours required for the audit (based on past audits, special information he may have, and the auditor's survey analysis). He also negotiates travel and other expenses. From the extension of the agreed upon hours and rate, plus travel, etc., he arrives at a maximum contract dollar amount.
- Executes a contract which includes:
  1. Statement that the audit is to be performed in accordance with the instruction booklet, which gives details on audit objectives, audit standards, certain required audit procedures, and a desired long-form audit report format.
  2. Maximum contract amount and method of billing.
  3. Agreement that he will make a review of the audit upon receipt of a rough draft of the report.
  4. Delivery date.
- Notifies the agency by letter of the official assignment of the accounting firm.
- Maintains a liaison and overall supervisory role during the course of the audit, which may include attendance at the exit conference.
- Obtains a copy of the draft of the auditor's report, along with copies of the audit program, internal control survey, and any special questionnaires, etc. which he might have asked for that year. He reviews this material. In the review he utilizes, but does not restrict himself to, a checklist based on the instruction booklet and other special instructions.
- Meets with the firm, discusses review findings, examines work papers when necessary, and comes to an agreement on changes to be made in the report and occasionally on the need for more field work.
- Reads the final report when it is received in order to see that action agreed to in previous meetings has been taken, that there are no factual or typographical errors, and that no obvious changes have been made from the rough draft text.
- Distributes the report, with a transmittal letter in which the Auditor General concurs or does not concur with the findings and recommendations.
- Appears before the Legislative Audit Commission, with the accounting firm if necessary, to assist in their review of the report. The auditee is usually present.

Governmental Operational Audits By Private Accounting Firms

Chester E. Nelson, Jr., CPA

The Internal Auditor Mar./April 1974

In the past four years, the North Dakota Legislative Council has contracted with private accounting firms to conduct operational audits or "performance reviews" of state agencies. The reviews have been well received by members of the Legislature and have resulted in significant changes in departmental operations.

The definition of an operational audit for our purposes is similar to that of the Comptroller General of the United States in his publication entitled "Standards of Audit of Governmental Organizations, Programs, Activities and Functions."

North Dakota's experience with operational auditing on an experimental basis indicates:

- Private accounting firms are able to meet the challenge of conducting operational audits.
- The success of the operational audit is in part dependent upon its acceptance by the management of the department.
- The acceptance by the Legislature of the final audit report and subsequent legislative action is primarily dependent upon the degree of legislator involvement in the audit.

A number of accounting firms have expressed interest in and demonstrated an ability to perform operational audits for the state. Success has been achieved in contracting with both national and regional accounting firms. Since some firms are experienced in operational auditing for private industry, the transition to governmental work comes quite easily for them. The work of the General Accounting Office through the American Institute of Certified Public Accountants and the inclusion of operational auditing or performance auditing in a number of regional seminars and programs open to private firms has had a profound impact in the development of private firms' capabilities to do the work.

If an accounting firm is not familiar with operational auditing, the state provides them with copies of articles, publications, and other materials, and gives them a considerable amount of direction, advice and consultation during the engagement.

After a state department has been selected for an operational audit, the auditor and the legislative committee must develop a positive relationship with that department. This phase of the work must not be underrated. As one has observed: "Help is never really help unless and until it is perceived as 'helpful' by the person on the receiving end – regardless of the good intention or reputation of the helper or consultant."

To be successful, the auditor and the committee and its staff must be able to convey to the agency to be audited that they are as sincerely interested in helping the organization as any good doctor is in helping his patient. People in state top management generally are not deluded. They can sense objectivity, honesty, and — above all — integrity.

To establish this relationship to the point where the department is receptive to the engagement and the final audit report, departmental top management must be shown that the auditor will work under the following guidelines:

- The review is made with the purpose of improving future operations; therefore unnecessary criticism of the past will be avoided.
- Reference will be made to procedures, practices, and activities, rather than personalities — to the extent possible.
- The auditor will analyze his findings taking into consideration the constraints and circumstances faced by management and the crucial dynamics of internal power and politics underlying and intermingled with the organization's functional operations.
- The auditor will be objective and give management an opportunity to express its point of view or justification for handling a situation a certain way and will accept that viewpoint when, upon objective analysis, it proves to be a sound approach to the problem.
- The audit is geared toward helping the department establish an improved level of communications with the Legislature.

Now that a good working relationship has been established with the department, how is legislative support to implement report recommendations obtained? Legislative support is dependent upon the degree of the lawmakers' involvement during the audit. Consequently, to the degree the legislators get involved in the audit; to that same degree will they most likely accept the responsibility to sponsor and support legislation to implement the audit recommendations.

Legislative committees should have the opportunity to hear a number of interim reports from the auditors on the progress of the audit, and to hear department heads make the appropriate responses to recommendations and findings included in such preliminary reports. Once this is done, the legislature's understanding of the department, its activities, and its problems will be substantial.

Encourage legislators to ask questions to satisfy concerns which they might have regarding the departmental activities. The auditor's reply to such questions is an important phase of the audit.

Any additional effort by the auditor to respond to legislator, legislative staff, or departmental top management concern or inquiry, contributes to the willingness of legislators and department personnel to accept responsibility to support the implementation of the audit recommendations.

The state's operational audit reports are not only the culmination of much effort on the part of the auditors or consultants, but the final report also represents contributions by many other people, each of whom has a feeling of responsibility for at least a portion of the report.

Rotation and Selection of External Auditing Firms

Lyle D. Botkin

The Internal Auditor Nov./Dec. 1973

The rotation of accounting firms means that a city will change firms after a set period of years. It should be noted, however, that with rotation, the same accounting firm will be called upon again when the rotation pattern of those firms interested in doing the audit has turned a full cycle. One question facing cities is whether to retain the same accounting firm on an indefinite basis or to rotate accounting firms. If a city adopts a policy of rotating accounting firms, then for what period of time should the same firm be retained?

Method of Rotation and Selection

The City of Wichita is under a Commission-Manager form of government and each year the City Commission selects an accounting firm to do the annual audit and any other special audits that may be required as a result of administering federal and state grants. It has been the city's long term policy to have a three year rotation of accounting firms provided their performances as auditors are satisfactory. Rotation terms vary from two to five years generally.

It is my personal opinion that Wichita would receive equal or better quality services and objectivity from its accounting firms if they were to retain them for a period of five years, thereby allowing each accounting firm to spread the initial cost of the audit over a longer period of time. This would result in lower overall costs and superior performance and efficiencies.

A notice of request for the annual audit proposal is mailed to all local CPA firms declared eligible by the Wichita Chapter of Certified Public Accountants.

Firms wishing to participate in the audit submit a letter expressing their interest within a specified time period. The letters are then submitted to the City Commission. After the selection has been made, a contract is entered into with the successful CPA firm and approved by the City Commission.

Arguments for Rotation

- It is politically expedient to rotate accounting firms when there is more than one qualified accounting firm in a city expressing an interest in doing the audit.
- By rotating accounting firms, the independent CPAs will be working with the knowledge that their firm's work will itself be subject to examination by those firms who come after them. This results in greater attention, application, and objectivity in the audit. Under this method, a city receives better service and becomes involved in a wider exchange of views because of contact with more than one CPA firm.
- If a CPA firm is selected on a permanent basis there is some danger that it may become too familiar with a city's problems and personnel will unconsciously lose complete objectivity. This of course depends

on the CPA firm's policy of personnel rotation and on the audit itself.

- There is less chance of collusion arising between the city employees and the audit staff or among employees because of the threat of future examinations by other CPA firms.
- The auditor's independence may be strengthened by the rotation of accounting firms. The entire community of taxpayers and administration is dependent upon a high degree of independence.

Arguments Against Rotation

- There is a possibility that rotation may involve a change to less competent CPAs which would be detrimental to the city. However, if this were to happen, the city would still be able to retain other auditors since the contracts are normally for only one year at a time and the administration must renew its approval annually.
- There is much to learn about a city's past history before a qualified audit can be performed, therefore, the city may not get as good a service as it would by retaining the same firm. Furthermore, the start-up or first-time-through cost of a new auditor will cost more over the period of association.
- There is a possibility that as a city adopts a rotation policy, the larger firms with more influential connections than those of smaller firms would in effect corner the market and a wide distribution of audit engagements would not be attained. However, in employing an accounting firm to perform an audit of a city, certainly consideration should be given to the firm's qualifications and abilities to perform such an audit.
- By rotating accounting firms, the auditor may cease to take as lively an interest in the city's affairs if his firm would not be engaged the following year. This is a weak argument because it fails to consider that the CPA firm may be called upon in future years under the rotation plan.

Rotation Recommended

There are many advantages that a city would gain by engaging the same accounting firm over a long period of time. However, the advantages of rotation of accounting firms outweigh the arguments against rotation. It is through rotation of accounting firms that a city brings in new blood and an alertness which provides better service and advice. Rotation also tends to insure the auditor's independence to the public. Lack of competency of available auditors is one of the most valid reasons for a non-rotation policy.

The audit committee concept is applicable to cities and might include two members from a city's elected governing body and two or more full-time city personnel. Use of an audit committee should help insure that qualified auditors would be selected who have the necessary skills to audit computerized records and other records requiring particular specialized abilities and thereby help prevent an "Equity Funding" from occurring in the city government.

The increased costs from rotating a city's accounting firms is a small price to pay for greater objectivity. The decision that a city has to make as to what period of years it should retain the same accounting firm certainly has a direct bearing on both the worth and cost of the audits.

Independence of the Government Auditor's Position in the Political Organization

Hugh Dorrian, CPA

The Internal Auditor Sept./Oct. 1975

By the very nature of the position, the auditor of a municipality is an objective reviewer of the city's financial transactions. The auditor's function in most municipalities is twofold. First, he is the chief accounting officer of the governmental unit. Second, he is responsible for the actual audit function. In general, the auditor is not responsible for making policy decisions regarding which course of action a governmental unit should pursue. Instead, his function is to insure that whichever course of action is chosen is in fact carried out within the legal constraints set forth.

It is imperative that the auditor maintain independence and professional standards in the performance of his various functions. This may appear to be difficult to accomplish since the auditor must operate in the local political system. In Columbus, Ohio, as in many cities, the auditor occupies an elected post. The dichotomy of political survival and maintenance of professionalism would seem to be a difficult one to reconcile.

The Columbus experience, however, has not borne this out. The fact that the city auditor is an elected official has not traditionally affected the professional standing of the position. Since the adoption of the charter in 1914, relatively few persons have held the position of city auditor. This fact stands as testimony to the low political volatility of the position. Thus, one could conclude that the political constraints have had a negligible effect on the auditor in terms of his professional performance.

The position of the auditor should also be examined from the point of view of his day-to-day relationships with the existing departments and divisions within the governmental hierarchy and with the increasing number of private and quasi-public agencies. It is imperative that the auditor establish a close working relationship with these subunits of government while maintaining a high degree of independence and professionalism in his dealings with these groups. His position is much like that of the umpire who must carefully guard his association with individual ball players. How does one protect this delicate position?

Preaudit and Postaudit Functions

In performing the preaudit function, it is mandatory that consistency of decisions exist. Standardized office procedures for the handling of routine transactions should be spelled out whenever feasible. Explicit procedures substantially reduce unnecessary discretionary judgments on the part of the staff auditor handling the individual transaction. Furthermore, standard procedures clarify to each department the course of action that may be expected in any particular instance. Explicit procedures lend themselves to the integrity of the fiscal decision-making process.

Now, attention will be shifted to the performance of the postaudit function. Within the past few years, the auditor's dominant function has evolved from performing preaudit verification only. The evolution has resulted in the contemporary auditor's finding himself in the position of an accountant and of a postauditor. This change of roles is primarily due to the dynamic increase in federal grants and third-party contracts. The standardization discussed earlier is less applicable in these areas due to the dynamics of the decision-making process.

Two Options for the Postaudit

In the performance of the postaudit function, the auditor has two basic options open to him. First, the audit may be performed by the internal staff or by an independent CPA firm. Columbus chose the latter course of action. This is consistent with the concepts of professionalism and independence of the auditor as it removes the audit one step further from the realm of political involvement.

There are several other factors which support the choice of the CPA option. First, the postaudit work load is not distributed evenly throughout the year. Peak-loading personnel would be costly and could not be used efficiently on a year-round basis. Utilization of independent CPA's also provides an intangible benefit to the contracting agency which is not often recognized. The fact that an independent professional is serving in a judgment capacity apart from the traditional environment of the governmental system helps in a significant measure to create a trustworthy relationship between the local government and the private agency. Agency directors and the staff tend to perform in a more creative and imaginative manner when an environment which minimizes the inherent bureaucracy of government and its process of "overseeing" its constituents is created.

Internal Audit in the Postaudit

One caveat of the use of independent CPA firms is that agencies sometimes desire a direct review by "city hall." Often this may be the only association the subunit may have with the formal hierarchy. An agency concerned with future funding may welcome a chance to prove their worthiness. An internal audit team will often act as the eyes and ears of the city, assimilating information in conjunction with the financial audit.

Columbus has handled this drawback by attempting to combine a nonfinancial review along with the CPA audit. Such a combination will aid the responsiveness of the city auditor to the demands of present-day fiscal decisions.

9
reporting

The end product of the audit process should be improvement in management; and the audit report is the means of accomplishing this. The report ties together the concept of the audit plan, the background surrounding the area being audited, management's plans and standards, the conditions as they exist, analysis of deviations uncovered, and recommendations to resolve problems or issues that have been identified. The report is a communication device intended to stimulate corrective action where it is called for.

The audit report also provides a means of discharging accountability by reporting to higher levels of management, and to the constituency, the faithfulness, efficiency, and effectiveness with which public officials have carried out the tasks for which they are responsible.

However, the audit report can also be a dynamic device that, properly composed, can motivate the auditee or the client to action. An aura of cooperative effort can be created if the report:

- Has a constructive tone
- Identifies corrective action that can improve deficiencies
- Is clear and brief
- Provides full disclosure
- Includes auditees' comments or positions
- Eliminates the immaterial information

Probably one of the most sensitive facets of the reporting process is the construction of the audit findings. These findings are the elements of the audit report and are the action items for both client and auditee. However, in order for proper action to be taken, both parties need basic information. To supply this information, auditors have generally agreed that certain items should be reported and discussed. These items are:

- Background information relative to the subject being reported
- References and standards that were established by the auditee or the auditor with the auditee
- Actual conditions that were found
- Deviations from the standards
- Results of the analyses made: basic cause, underlying cause, and the impact on the auditee's operations
- Recommendations for correcting deficiencies

The process of developing these findings by the field auditor results in a disciplined approach not only to writing the report but also to conducting the audit.

Disclosure, a controversial subject in today's audit community, is especially sensitive in the area of governmental auditing due to the position of auditors as officials of the government that is being reported on, even though they may be independent as to the auditee. Also, there are political and social repercussions resulting from full disclosure, especially when the audit reports are available to the public. Then, there is the auditee's defensive attitude resulting from full disclosure. This attitude can make it difficult to gain the auditee's cooperation in implementing audit recommendations. Nevertheless, full disclosure is a basic standard and must be adhered to, even though there are methods which can be used to minimize the sharpness of the impact.

Including the auditee's comments in the report is not only good audit reporting but often improves the auditor/auditee relationship. It is a good policy to give management a statement telling what the auditee has done or plans to do relative to the auditor's recommendations. Also, the auditee's negative positions should be given the same treatment as the auditor's positive statements. The auditee's opportunity to have a say in the matter results in better relationship and is a first step toward participative auditing.

Finally, the convention of materiality is essential. Audit reports filled with trivialities discredit the audit operation and reduce the credibility of reports. As a result, management may obtain information on operations by other methods which may not be as effective as well-performed audits.

The articles in this chapter are about report writing. Professor John A. Edds, Brock University, Ontario, talks about the "Importance of Report Writing." Dr. James E. Smith, College of William and Mary in Virginia, supplies a graphic piece on communication as it relates to internal auditing. Robert B. Brown, CPA, Washington, D.C., discusses disclosure in internal audit reports. Reporting auditee compliance is addressed by Dr. M. A. Dittenhofer, American University; and a companion piece on "Obtaining and Reporting Auditee Comments" is supplied by Robert J. Ryan, CPA, U.S. General Accounting Office.

The Importance of Report Writing

John A. Edds, CIA

The Internal Auditor Nov./Dec. 1975

Audit reports are not something to be dashed off between jobs. In fact the ability to write effective reports is a skill essential to successful audits. In a poll taken recently by the American Institute of CPA's, written and oral reports were ranked first in importance for the beginning CPA – out of a list of fifty-three subjects, both technical and nontechnical.

Essentials of Effective Reports

If you have done a thorough job of auditing, you should have something significant and worthwhile to say. This is the first and obvious requisite of good report-writing. Presumably, your findings are well thought out and documented and, having gathered together all the facts along with your own observations and opinions, you are now ready to tell your story. What you tell to whom will be determined largely by the purpose of the report – if not by the audit itself. The purpose will indicate which aspects of the assignment you should write about. Since managers today are literally deluged with reports – and even reports *on* reports – the auditor should strive to produce a report which is clear cut, easily understood, and leads the reader to a logical conclusion. Managers respond positively to a writing style which leads them to logical conclusions. It also encourages them to agree with the auditor's recommendations. Since managers don't usually have the time to wade through long reports, looking for the point to the whole thing, the auditor should cooperate by presenting his conclusions and recommendations at the very beginning.

Writing the Report

When you have started the actual writing of the report, you should keep in mind the following points to avoid many of the failings which are common to audit reports:

- Consider the reader's background and familiarity with technical jargon.
- Consider the use of photographs, charts, or diagrams.
- Use logic and judicious marshaling of facts instead of referring to "authorities" or to "generally accepted accounting principles."
- When referring to a standard procedure, either quote directly from the source or paraphrase in such a way so that the reader easily gets the gist of your reference.
- Possibly the most serious mistake is to criticize a particular practice without recommending an alternative approach to the problem.

Before drafting the report, the auditor may find it desirable, even necessary, to express some of his findings and recommendations in the form of a memorandum and to obtain management's acceptance, written or otherwise. Without allowing the project to drag on indefinitely, the auditor should attempt to have corrective action agreed to and initiated. A successful effort in this direction will pave the way for a report which deals with actual accomplishments; namely, the circumstances as he discovered them, his plan to correct or to improve these circumstances, and the action which has been taken so far in this regard. Also, if management disagrees with his conclusions and with his assessment of the situation, the auditor should make note of this when preparing the final draft of his report. However, he should be quite certain that there is no disagreement on the facts themselves and that his conclusions are stated clearly and are supported by objective arguments.

The Form of the Report

Most reports will tend to be organized along certain general lines, and it is worthwhile to consider the form of organization which is most common among audit reports.

The auditor should devote one section of his report to a summary of its entire contents. Many readers will obtain all the information they need from this summary. Those who require a more complete account of the audit will delve into the body of the report.

Following this general summary, there should be a series of separate sections arranged in some logical order with each section being devoted to one of the auditor's major findings along with his opinions or conclusions and his recommendations. In each section, sufficient background data should be provided so that even a reader who is not well acquainted with the situation under review can perceive the significance of the auditor's remarks.

The material for this digest was abstracted by Dale Knowles from J. Edds, *Auditing for Management* (Toronto, Ontario: Sir Isaac Pitman Ltd., 1971).

Communication, Internal Auditing, and You

Dr. James E. Smith, CPA

The Internal Auditor May/June 1974

Do you desire to communicate more efficiently, effectively, and influentially? If the answer is yes, advance to GO. Otherwise, select the STOP response.

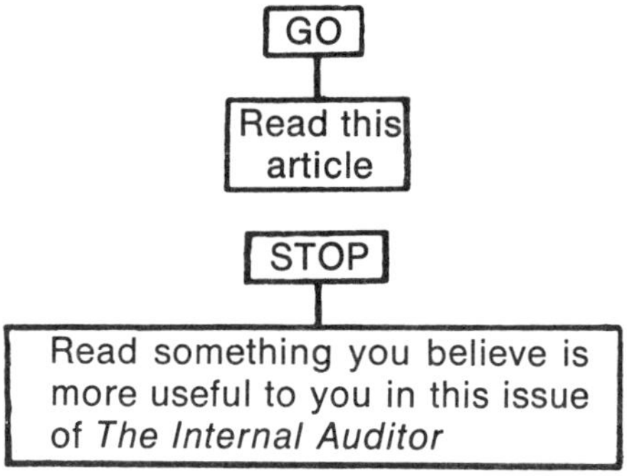
GO
Read this article
STOP
Read something you believe is more useful to you in this issue of The Internal Auditor

As an internal auditor, you are required to communicate with management, other members of your internal auditing staff, and with internal auditors outside your organization. The broadening of the internal auditing function (i.e., into operational or management auditing) has increased both the benefit and the necessity for you to achieve adequate communication.

The purposes of this article are three-fold.

1. To make you aware of the relevance of communication theory to your job.
2. To move you to exert the required effort to improve your communication attempts, both written and oral.
3. To provide you with insight into how you can develop a communication framework that will enable you to achieve the desired improvement.

SELECTED PRINCIPLES OF COMMUNICATION THEORY

A communication model.

The following communication theory model is useful in applying communication theory to any discipline.

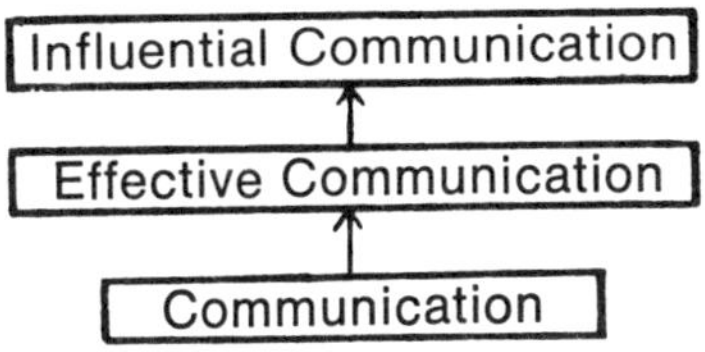

Communication occurs on three levels. First, simple communication can happen without its being either effective or influential. Second, effective communication can be achieved without its being influential. However, the third level – influential communication – cannot be attained unless simple and effective communication have first occurred.

For example, simple communication occurs when the person understands your message as you intend him to. When the receiver also feels the message is useful, your communication is effective. On the other hand, your communication is influential only when the individual receiving your message takes the action you wish him to.

Do you want to simply communicate or also make your report or message effective and influential? The choice is up to you.

FIELDS OF EXPERIENCE

A principle that demonstrates the value of communications theory is the field of experience of the information source and the destination. The source and destination can only encode and decode within their

FIELDS OF EXPERIENCE

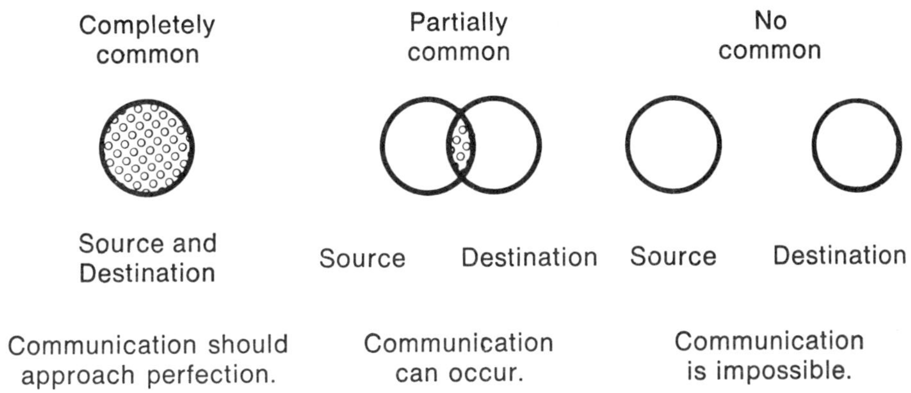

fields of experience. The larger the common field of experience of the source and the destination, the greater the probability that communication will result. The following diagrams illustrate the three fields of experience of the source and the destination and their effect upon communication.

APPLICATION OF MODEL AND SELECTED PRINCIPLES TO INTERNAL AUDITING

Below are some illustrations of how the principles of communications theory and the model can be applied by you.

1. Determine the objective (i.e., communication, effective communication, or influential communication) of your communication attempt. If you are trying to get an operating manager to modify an operating system, then you want to encode your message so that you will do more than merely have him understand your message.
2. Identify the destination, his information needs, and his field of experience. These requirements exist regardless of your objective.
3. Use terminology that is within his field of experience. It's better for you to learn operating terminology than expect management to understand your non-operating terminology. You will make a better impression on management and more likely achieve your objective.
4. Use specialized terminology only if it makes the destination's role easier. For example, the terms for the types of audits (i.e., financial and compliance, economy and efficiency, and program results) proposed by the Comptroller General can be functional or dysfunctional depending on the destination.
5. Define the substance of the term used rather than use a synonym, if the object of your communication does not understand the term originally used. Example: Do not define an operational audit as a management audit.
6. Use emotive terms only if they will be perceived by the destination in the manner you desire. Don't describe an audit of operational activities as a management audit if you know management is opposed to audits "of management."

Numerous other applications can be made based on only the two principles and the model, but space limitations do not permit doing so. A general framework of communication theory possesses tremendous potential for enabling you to improve your internal auditing function through improving your communication.

Disclosure in Operational Audits

Robert B. Brown, CPA

The Internal Auditor October 1976

Recently, there has been a tremendous amount of discussion in the press concerning disclosure by corporations of political and other payoffs. Many of these "revelations" concern the way U.S. businesses operate overseas.

There has been no lack of similar disclosures about domestic operations. These improprieties have also been found in government.

The *New York Times* recently reported that the head of the American Bankers Association called for greater disclosure by the U.S. banks to stem what he called an erosion of confidence in the banking system.

Accordingly, "sunshine" laws recently enacted around the country promise to allow public scrutiny of government activities.

The accounting profession itself has been embroiled in this problem. This is a result of the query "where were the auditors?" and the profession's responsibility to attest to financial statements and carry on traditional internal audit duties. A 1975 *Wall Street Journal* front-page headline read:

> *Agonizing Auditors . . . Accountants Reassess Disclosure Standards After Business Scandals . . . Bribes, Political Gifts Spur Debate on Which Items Must Be Held 'Material' . . . A Guardian of Morals?"*

Disclosure in Audit Reports

It is my view that the audit report is the end result of the disclosure process. It must be preceded, of course, by adequate field work and the decision to make a disclosure. As such, the report must contain all relevant, material information that will be required by its users. It must be in suitable detail and in a format that makes it easy to understand.

The disclosure problem is essentially a reporting problem. It is a problem that has been peculiar to financial audit. The problem was aggravated and perhaps caused by the fact that financial auditing is a reasonably well-defined but constantly changing structured process leading to one ultimate goal: the auditor's certification of the reasonableness of management's financial representations.

Information omitted or inadequately reported must be footnoted for purposes of full-disclosure. Much has been written about auditors' responsibilities — not only to the person paying for the audit but also to those who might depend on the attestations. I feel the crux of the issue is that financial audit reports in the public sector are not informative enough because of the nature of the public sector and because of the format of the traditional government financial report. The result is the continued growth and emphasis on operational auditing in government. The report user needs information.

Disclosure in Operational Audits

Operational audit reports are much less structured than financial audit reports. The universe is there to look at. The disclosure concept (or, what and how to report) could hardly be set down for an operational audit report. Government operations do not end up with a final profit or loss figure. What is to be reported on and fully described (disclosed) must lead to accomplishing one, several, or all of the purposes of governmental operational audits. They must determine the effectiveness, efficiency, and economy of operations.

Information on conflict of interest, spurious arrangements, uneconomical practices, and similar things that are not within the defined scope of financial audits, have always come within the accepted scope and disclosure of operational audits. The operational auditor is not hampered by a stylized reporting structure with stringent reporting requirements. Quality and the validity of what is to be reported are prerequisites. Nevertheless, disclosure in reports on operational audits can and should be done within some parameters.

The Privacy Act

The operational auditor would do well to become acquainted with the ramifications of the federal privacy acts. Full public disclosure (as opposed to in-house reporting) may conflict with the acts' provisions.

Leaving their interpretation to those in the legal profession, suffice it to say that such laws affect what can be disclosed in an operational audit report.

Materiality

Disclosure of an item in the operational audit report should be governed by its materiality or relative importance. This requirement in operational auditing is important because of the amount of available trivia which, if reported, would encumber the report and make it a worthless laundry list of unimportant information. The auditor should establish materiality guidelines for the staff. These guidelines should show how to write a report that is a crisp, concise, and factual recitation of important issues for management. Materiality is the quality that identifies the items considered necessary to management's understanding and correction of the problem.

Conclusion

I believe there are a few steps that need to be reemphasized by the operational auditor to assure that he is complying with the spirit of full disclosure. First: identify management's standards and policies on codes of conduct and financial disclosure requirements for senior staff. Second: firm up the working relationships with your organization's legal and investigatory staff. Third: make your staff increase its vigilance, and give it the latest information on all aspects of white-collar crime. Finally: be certain that the information in your reports has been developed according to appropriate governmental audit standards.

Reporting Auditee Compliance

Dr. Mortimer A. Dittenhofer, CIA

The Internal Auditor October 1976

One of the basic objectives of internal audit is to achieve better management through actions that correct conditions disclosed by the audit report. Thus, it is important that this corrective action, whether accomplished or in process, be identified and commented upon.

There are several reasons for this. Advising management that the action to correct a deficiency is being taken is part of staff work. Through acknowledging that the corrective action has been, or is being taken, operating management is given credit for promptly correcting deficiencies. In addition, through this type of reporting, top management is made aware that there *was* a deficiency even though steps have been taken to correct it.

Opinions of Responsible Officials

The accompanying article by Robert J. Ryan of the General Accounting Office explains how the audit report should handle the views of responsible officials. This aspect complements the corrective action. If responsible officials do not concur in the finding but institute the action recommended by the auditor, management should be told. Obviously, when the auditee does not concur with the recommendation or the finding, the report should say why.

Reporting Details

It is important that the report clearly identify the corrective action that was taken. The description of the corrective action should be in as much detail as was used in the description of the surface and basic causes of the deficiency. The auditor should:

- state the corrective action
- identify who is responsible for that action
- indicate the time frame (when it will be completed)
- describe how the corrective action will remedy both the surface causes and the basic or underlying causes

Where higher authority was required to effect the action, this information and how it was accomplished should also be reported. This section of the report should close with a statement of whether the auditor has observed the corrective action or set up a time for a follow-up check. This will make sure that:

- the action has been taken
- the unsatisfactory condition has been remedied

Participative Auditing

The clear description of corrective action taken by the auditee, especially when the auditor acknowledges that the investigation was recommended or assisted by the auditee, is a characteristic of participative auditing. This is a new development that engenders a cooperative and positive attitude on the part of the auditee and a greater commitment to working out adequate solutions.

A Word of Caution

The auditor should be aware of situations in which the auditee glibly agrees to corrective action as soon as a deficiency is uncovered. Action such as this may be taken by the auditee in order to preclude continued investigation that would disclose further deficiencies and possibly malfeasance. The auditor should not be so enamored with the possibility of reporting that corrective action was taken that he is willing to curtail investigation based on the auditee's word that the situation will be corrected.

Disagreement With Corrective Action

Although this article deals with reporting when corrective action *has* been taken, the article would not be complete without stating that there are some deficiencies where a corrective action would not be practical under current conditions. If this situation does arise, the auditor should identify the condition and express an opinion on materiality and practicality of corrective action.

Conclusion

Continuous cooperation and understanding between the auditor and the auditee is necessary in order to convince the auditee of the desirability of making changes. It is in the best interests of the organization to have the auditee make the necessary changes voluntarily. The tone and content of the audit report should state this condition even when the auditee must research and determine the necessary action.

The result will be an informed management, a satisfied auditee, a more efficient and effective operation, and a happy auditor.

Obtaining and Reporting Auditee Comments

Robert J. Ryan, CPA

The Internal Auditor October 1976

When an auditor audits financial statements, he usually does not have to obtain overall comments from the officials of the audited entity and include these in his report. The auditor does, of course, obtain evidence and support for an opinion and makes decisions about the necessary range and depth of audit coverage by obtaining comments from officials of the auditee during the course of the audit. These are not usually included in the report, however.

Comments on Broad-Scope Audits

In expanding the audit process to include a review of economy, efficiency (operational or management auditing), and effectiveness (evaluation of program results), the auditor delves into areas where more judgment must be used. In many cases, the client usually has officials and employees whose experience and expertise make them capable of rendering informed judgments on how and why procedures are followed and whether desired results are being obtained.

This is not to say that they can evaluate such matters in the same light as an independent auditor. But their opinions and reactions to the auditor's findings and conclusions should be considered.

Early Discussions of Reports

Tentative findings which may involve significant deficiencies should be discussed as early as possible with appropriate officials of the audited organization. This is beneficial to the orderly development of the findings and should normally result in reduced audit efforts and less processing time for the draft and final reports. Such early discussions also provide the auditor with a better understanding of the situations discussed and enable the auditor to make suggestions for improvements.

In addition, when the report is drafted, the auditor should provide a copy to auditee officials and request their advance reviews and comments. This lets those who may be affected adversely by the auditor's report have their "day in court." It gives them an opportunity to state what they think about the auditor's findings and conclusions and say what they intend to do about them.

After the auditee's comments are obtained, they must be evaluated. Are they responsive to the findings? If not, further efforts should be made through the auditee's officials in order to obtain reponsive comments.

Reporting the Auditee's Comments

According to the government audit standards[1], the audit report should:

> *Include recognition of the views of responsible officials of the organization, program, function, or activity audited on the auditor's findings, conclusions, and recommendations. Except where the possibility of fraud or other compelling reason may require different treatment, the auditor's tentative findings and conclusions should be reviewed with such officials. When possible, without undue delay, their views should be obtained in writing and objectively considered and presented in preparing the final report.*

Methods of Presenting Auditee's Comments

Auditee's comments should be appropriately recognized in the final report. This may be done in at least two ways. The comments may be included with each finding as a separate subsection before the auditor's recommendations. They may also be included as an appendix to the report. Either way, the auditor should refer to the comments in presenting the findings, conclusions, and recommendations.

The auditor should clearly indicate agreement or disagreement with the auditee's comments. In some cases, the auditor may revise the report after considering the auditee's comments. If significant changes are made, the auditee

[1]The Comptroller General of the United States, *Standards for Audit of Governmental Organizations, Programs, Activities, & Functions*, The Comptroller General of the United States (1972), p. 8.

should be given another opportunity to comment.

In other cases, the auditor may not believe that the opposing comments are valid. The auditor must then effectively state his position by rebutting the auditee's comments in the report and thoroughly documenting his rebuttal. In supporting the rebuttal, the auditor may find the comments valid and drop a finding or modify a position.

When the auditee concurs with the findings, this tends to support their validity. When this occurs, the auditee usually indicates that corrective action has either been taken or promised. This should be presented, as appropriate, in the report.

The auditor may consider not including the auditee's written comments in the report if they are voluminous. In such cases, the auditor should include those comments that are most responsive and significant.

When the Auditee Does Not Comment

If advance review and comments are not received from the auditee, the auditor should give the reason in the report. Perhaps the auditor did not request comments. The auditee might have refused to comment or delayed too long.

If comments were not requested by the auditor, the reasons for not doing so should be stated. This could, for example, be due to possible effects on pending legal actions.

Recently, I have noted that some executive departments refuse to comment on the auditor's draft reports. They prefer to await the auditor's final report before stating their position. In such cases, the auditor may find it necessary to issue a second "final report" to deal with the comments.

In any case, if the auditee does not respond to the auditor's request for comments, or when the delay in receiving the auditee's comments makes it necessary to issue the report without them, the report should clearly describe the auditor's efforts to obtain such comments.

10
special issues

Four articles that didn't seem to fit anyplace else but which were too important to omit are in this chapter. The first one relates a case in which the New York courts upheld the concept of operational auditing. It is probably the most important single article in the collection. Written by Martin Ives, then deputy comptroller of New York State and now deputy comptroller of New York City, it tells about a challenge that was intended to limit New York State auditing to pure financial postaudit activity.

The second article by Director Donald L. Scantlebury, U.S. General Accounting Office, describes the intergovernmental audit forums. These forums started in 1973 and are composed of federal, state, and local audit officials. The objective of the forums is to discuss and resolve intergovernmental audit issues before they become problems and to advance the state of the auditing art by an exchange of ideas from the three levels of government.

Frank M. Olmstead, CPA, a progressive former state auditor from New Mexico, describes the state audit organization's successful efforts to resolve conflicts between the legislative and executive factions of the state. He also describes how he was able to modernize what had been a traditional financial audit operation in the face of opposition from parties at interest in the state.

The last article by Dr. Robert J. Freeman, University of Alabama, puts together an epilogue entitled "Internal Auditing in the State and Local Governments: Poised for Takeoff." Written in 1973, the article challenged The Institute of Internal Auditors to become the catalyst in the modernization of auditing at the nonfederal levels. Interestingly enough, the article foretold the advances that have come about in the four years following its publication.

Courts Uphold Operational Auditing In New York State

Martin Ives, CIA, CPA

The Internal Auditor July/Aug. 1974

In a landmark decision, New York State's highest court has upheld the right of the State Comptroller to conduct operational audits of the state's public authorities. The 1973 decision added the weight of the judiciary to the growing movement among governmental agencies in extending the concept of audit to embrace not only financial accountability, but also performance efficiency and effectiveness in accomplishing program goals.

Public authorities have been created by all levels of government to undertake such projects as the construction and operation of toll roads, bridges, airports and port facilities; the construction of governmental office buildings and public housing; and the development of commercial and industrial facilities. As a general rule, they finance construction through the issuance of revenue bonds, operate and maintain the facilities, and collect tolls and fees sufficient to finance day-to-day operations and repay the borrowings. Although public authorities are generally intended to be self-sufficient, many have received substantial government support in recent years through operating subsidies, construction grants, and interest-free loans.

Public Authorities Play Major Role

Taken as a group, the public authorities play a major role in administering governmental and quasi-governmental activities in New York State. The 36 statewide public authorities had aggregate assets of $15.4 billion, outstanding borrowings of $10.6 billion, and gross revenues of $1.6 billion in 1972.

Audit Monitors Activities of Public Authorities

Audit by the State Comptroller provides one of major means by which New York State monitors the activities of its public authorities. The New York State Public Authorities Law, Section 2503 provides that: "... the state comptroller shall, from time to time but no less than once in every five years, examine the books and accounts of every authority . . ., including its receipts, disbursements, contracts, leases, sinking funds, investments and any other matters relating to its financial standing ..."

Shortly after the State Comptroller commenced audit of the New York City Transit Authority, it became evident that authority management would not provide all the records necessary for the Comptroller to conduct an audit in accordance with his standards. (The New York City Transit Authority, with expenditures of more than $700 million in fiscal year 1973, is responsible for operating the city's subway system and much of its surface transit.) The Comptroller thereupon decided to subpoena certain specific records.

Wide Audit Sought

The records subpoenaed by the Comptroller will provide some insight into the scope of the audit.

Among the items subpoenaed were reports and documents related to: the purchase of materials under a special maintenance program, the ability of the storerooms to fill requisitions, the establishment of labor productivity standards and comparisons of actual performance with the standards, departmental operating procedures, the evaluation of contractor performance in acquiring facilities, and the "on-time performance" of the surface and subway operations.

The Comptroller argued in his brief that such an audit was consistent with: his constitutional and statutory authority; legislative intent, both past and present; good auditing practices; accepted standards of governmental auditing; and his long established construction of the Comptroller's responsibilities to ascertain "not only that the books balance, but also that the public receives a dollar's value for every dollar spent." In support of this argument, the Comptroller cited the "Statement of Responsibilities of the Internal Auditor"; the General Accounting Office "Standards for Audit of Governmental Organizations, Programs, Activities and Functions"; the state's appropriation acts wherein the appropriation for audit of state agencies and public authorities is entitled "Management Audit Program"; and studies leading to the fixing of the Comptroller's audit responsibilities under the law.

Court Rules in Favor of Wide Audit

The Appellate Division, ruling in favor of the State Comptroller, noted that the courts in New York State have been extremely liberal in construing legislation designed to provide a system of financial checks and balances, particularly in the area of governmental agencies and public authorities. Citing a staff report which led to the adoption of the statute calling for audit of the public authorities, the Court suggested that the Comptroller's audit function "consists of more than a mere verification of financial accounts and balance sheets." Finally, the Court pointed out the Comptroller's approach to auditing was consistent with the scope of governmental audits in general, as described in the General Accounting Office Standards for Audit (Matter of Ronan v. Levitt, 42 A.D. 2d 10, 244 N.Y.S. 2d 624, 1973; motion for leave to appeal denied, 33 N.Y. 2d 514, 1973).

At the time this article was written (and subsequent to the Court decision), the State Comptroller had issued several interim audit reports based upon examination of the New York City Transit Authority. The subjects covered by these reports included inventory controls, overtime practices, procurement of certain commodities, and various aspects of labor utilization. Following is a brief summation of some of the audit conclusions:

- There is a need for improved supervision and for the development of better work standards in the surface maintenance department. Productivity of the Transit Authority surface maintenance department, when measured in terms of maintenance hours per bus, was approximately 50 percent below that of comparable private carriers.
- Substantial savings could be achieved through the develop-

ment of better manning schedules for the subway station booths.

- Savings of about $200,000 a year are possible in the acquisition and disposition of railroad ties. (This conclusion was developed through a comparison of the Authority's procedures with the procedures of comparable organizations.)
- There is a need for improved inventory management. The audit showed significant buildups of inventories that were not required in the reasonably foreseeable future.

Operational Auditing Stands Test

Thus, the concept of governmental operational auditing in New York State has stood the test of judicial review. The decision should help to further the development of operational auditing in governmental agencies throughout the nation. The reference in the decision to the audit standards adopted by the General Accounting Office should also lend further weight to the force of these standards.

A New Arrival — The Interagency Audit Forum

Donald L. Scantlebury, CIA, CPA

The Internal Auditor Nov./Dec. 1973

On July 25, 1973, a new organization called the Intergovernmental Audit Forum had its charter meeting. The organization is composed of top audit officials of 16 Federal agencies, 6 state auditors and 6 chief auditors of local governments.

The Federal members include all the grant-making Federal agencies plus representatives from the General Accounting Office, the General Services Administration, the Office of Management and Budget, and the Department of the Treasury.

The state members were selected by the Council of State Governments and include the state auditors from Maryland, Tennessee, Wisconsin, Illinois, Colorado, and Georgia.

Similarly, the local government auditors are being selected by the Municipal Finance Officers Association and include Baltimore, Maryland; San Diego, California; and Columbus, Ohio; as well as three other municipalities yet to be selected.

Who needs such an organization? To answer this, let's go back to its genesis.

In the Fall of 1972, a group of state auditors representing the Post-Audit Workshop of the National

Legislative Conference visited the Comptroller General, head of the General Accounting Office, to discuss with him some audit problems that had an intergovernmental implication.

These problems related to increasing demands made upon state auditors by the Federal Government in connection with the increases in special purpose grants in recent years and in anticipation of demands to be made under revenue sharing, then under consideration in the Congress.

A serious problem to the state auditors was that the Federal Government did not speak with one voice. They faced a myriad of different auditing requirements and had no one to turn to in the Federal Government to resolve conflicts and problems.

The Intergovernmental Audit Forum was what ultimately was conceived to help alleviate these problems.

What are its avowed purposes? Basically, to serve as a forum – a well chosen word – where auditors from the three levels of Government can meet, discuss mutual problems and hopefully resolve them. The Forum will have no authority to make decisions on its own.

The premise underlying the Forum is that if reasonable men get together and discuss their common problems, most of such problems can be readily resolved by action on the part of those involved without any need for a referee. The Forum, therefore, is a place to meet, discuss and agree on solutions.

Other purposes are to support the *Standards for Audit of Governmental Organizations, Programs, Activities and Functions* issued by the Comptroller General and to provide information as to how they are being implemented, problems created, and results achieved.

How will it operate? The Forum will meet at least quarterly and will consider issues raised by members, by regional forums which it hopes will be established in each of the ten Federal regions, or by others who wish to bring problems to the attention of the Forum.

When necessary, committees will consider specific problems. Committees specified in the charter include a committee on federally-assisted programs, auditor training and professional development, practices and standards, and an executive committee.

The Elected Auditor in New Mexico

Frank M. Olmstead, CPA

The Internal Auditor Jan./Feb. 1974

New Mexico's three cultures – Indian, Spanish, and so-called Anglo – and their occasional clashes have contributed to the state's colorful history. The history of post-auditing in New Mexico is as varied and tumultuous as the state's own history. Today's skirmishes are often fought in the halls and chambers of the legislature and the offices of the state's elected officials. When I assumed office in January 1971, I found a chaotic condition that reflected the battles between the legislative and the executive branches of the state government.

State Auditing History

Until 1957 the state comptroller, appointed by the governor, had directed post-auditing for the state. The elected state auditor had pre-audit duties only. In 1957, the legislature created the Department of Finance and Administration (DFA); abolished the position of state comptroller; and transferred the post-auditing duties to the elected state auditor.

Also in 1957, the legislature created the Legislative Finance Committee (LFC), a standing committee with members from both houses, which has the power to review the budget requests of selected state agencies, departments, and institutions, as well as their operation and management. The LFC also examines laws governing the finances and operation of state agencies and may recommend such changes in the law as it deems necessary.

It soon became apparent to members of the LFC that audit reports emanating from the office of the state auditor were simply a rehash of the agencies' financial transactions.

In 1965, the legislature established the Legislative Audit Commission and transferred to it all post-auditing duties.

Importance of State Auditor

However, the Supreme Court, in a decision handed down in 1968, ruled that the statute creating the Legislative Audit Commission was unconstitutional in that it sought to abolish by statute a constitutional office. In that decision, the Supreme Court defined the importance of the state auditor as an *elected* official:

> "It would seem to us that, both historically and fundamentally, the office of state auditor was created and exists for the basic purpose of having a completely independent representative of the people, accountable to no one else, with the power, duty, and authority to examine and pass upon the activities of state officers and agencies who, by law, receive and expend public money."

The Supreme Court decision also restored post-auditing duties to the state auditor's office.

The period from 1968 to 1970 saw a competent Republican auditor (a CPA) facing an unfriendly Democrat-controlled legislature. His salary was set at $2,500 below that of other executive officers. His budget, also, was ridiculously low.

Legislature Antagonistic

Upon assuming office in January 1971, I found the legislature generally antagonistic toward the state auditor. In a letter to the chairman of the Senate Finance Committee dated March 10, 1971, I described the situation in my office as follows:

- A critical lack of communications with independent auditing firms conducting audits of state agencies, caused by inadequate review procedures by my office and a lack of rules and guidelines for the independent accountants to follow.
- A serious delinquency in the completion of audits and particularly the audits of the major state agencies.
- A staff shortage of experienced auditors at the supervisory level.
- A profusion of audit reports that are not responsive to the needs of the legislature because they are directed primarily to fiscal affairs and do not report on compliance with law, nor upon the operations of the agencies.

My first year in office was frustrating because our budget was limited, the LFC was antagonistic, and the independent auditors were not conducting the types of audits we wanted. We did, however, conduct some audits for the LFC – a rather unique operation for an elected auditor.

New Audit Manual

One communications channel opened when the New Mexico State Society of Certified Public Accountants created a Committee on Relations with the State Auditor. We submitted a draft of our new manual, *Instructions for Performing Audits of Agencies of the State of New Mexico*, to this committee and to the registered public accountants (RPAs). The revised manual incorporated their suggestions.

The manual requires that each audit report include a section entitled "Accountant's Observations and Recommendations." Here, the auditor must disclose conditions relating to: 1) revenue and expenditures; 2) financial records, reporting, and budgetary controls; 3) internal accounting controls; 4) reconciliation with fiscal offices; 5) compliance with statutes, laws, rules, and regulations; 6) prior-year findings and recommendations; 7) significant variations in financial accounts; 8) fraud and dishonesty; and 9) efficiency in financial operations and management. As a result, our audit reports have been more informative and, therefore, more useful to the legislature.

Audits Bring Results

Our first operational audit pointed out glaring weaknesses in our public purchases act. Our preliminary studies of the state universities have shown that much work is needed in this area.

The end result has been that the LFC has appreciated our efforts and has encouraged us to continue to upgrade and improve our operations. Our budget was increased from $327,280 for the year ended June 30, 1971 to $604,984 for the current fiscal year. Of that amount, $78,117 was earmarked for operational audits to be performed at the request of the LFC.

Lack of Continuity — A Weakness

Our greatest remaining weakness is the lack of continuity in the office. The constitution limits the auditor to a single four-year term. (My term expires December 31, 1974.) Since the state constitution fails to specify any qualifications for this office, there is a question in the minds of LFC members as to what will happen when a new auditor is elected.

We proposed a constitutional amendment to create a legislative auditor, but the amendment was defeated by a legislative committee during the 1973 session.

We were then asked to submit to the LFC a plan that would promote continuity in the state's post-auditing needs. We suggested that financial and compliance audits should remain the responsibility of the elected state auditor, who would continue to be the principal auditor. It was also recommended that a legislative agency be created to conduct audits to analyze economy, efficiency, and program results in the various state agencies. The LFC is presently studying this plan.

Elected Auditors Can Be Effective

My own experiences lead me to believe that an elected auditor can establish an effective relationship with the legislature if he will 1) maintain a highly trained audit staff and 2) provide audit reports that meet the legislature's need for information about the effectiveness and efficiency of state agency operations.

Internal Auditing in the State and Local Governments: Poised for Takeoff

Dr. Robert J. Freeman, CPA

The Internal Auditor Mar./April 1973

A cursory review of internal auditing in state and local governments is apt to leave one pessimistic. Internal auditing is woefully underdeveloped here. Where provided for, it is often limited to preaudit of expenditure vouchers for clerical accuracy and legality. Furthermore, staff entry and retention requirements may be lax, salaries low, and professional development and advancement opportunities limited.

Poised For Takeoff

Yet I am optimistic on its prospects. In fact, I am convinced that internal auditing is "poised for takeoff" in state and local governments.

Significant change in any area of government requires the concurrent presence of numerous socio-political forces and technical competencies. However, these are but subsets of two fundamental prerequisites: (1) the need for the advancement must be recognized, and its achievement actively sought, by those commanding the necessary political and economic resources; and (2) the state of the art must be sufficiently advanced to permit the progress. These crucial prerequisites are now being met – thus we are entering an era of unparalleled potential for developing internal auditing in our state and local governments.

Need Recognition

The need for improved governmental management and accountability is gaining recognition at the state and local level. The effects of the "accountability" movement are clear: (1) legislatures, pressured by the public, are demanding better management and accountability from the executive branch; and (2) executive branch members, in response to legislative demands, are insisting upon better management and accountability for their subordinates. Demand for improved internal auditing soars in this situation.

Encouragement is also coming from the federal government. The present administration is seeking to strengthen state and local members of the federal-state-local partnership. Too, federal audit agencies are committed to developing viable federal-state-local audit networks and relying more upon both internal and external audits performed by or for state and local governments. Finally, forthcoming revenue sharing accountability requirements should add impetus to the demand for better internal auditing in state and local governments.

The State Of The Art

The state of the art can support both the initial demands for advancement and a sustained effort toward upgrading internal auditing within state and local government. Consider some of the factors indicative of this:

- *Experience.* Several outstanding internal audit groups have been developed in state and local governments. These have demonstrated its feasibility and garnered valuable implementation experience.
- *Competence.* Observe that (1) approaches, procedures, and manuals developed to date provide guidance and springboards for further development; (2) approaches and progressive ideas are being shared through speeches, articles, and conferences at an unprecedented rate; (3) training materials are becoming available; and (4) personnel are being exchanged among governments, and federal audit agencies are establishing intergovernmental assistance staffs.
- *Standards.* The IIA has developed standards for internal auditors, and has adopted a certification program. Too, the *Standards for Audit of Governmental Organizations, Programs, Activities and Functions* issued by the U.S. Comptroller General are applicable to state and local government internal audits.
- *Research and Development.* Relevant pure and applied research is underway. In addition, university business schools are recognizing the importance of the business of

government and adjusting their roles accordingly, and several major independent CPA firms are preparing for expanded audit and management services engagements with state and local governments. Such developments will have positive "spillover" effects on governmental internal auditing.

Needed: IIA Catalyst

Though "poised for takeoff," without catalytic action the potential for internal auditing in state and local government may remain untapped. Even worse, it may be implemented with fanfare but without proper planning and guidance – in form without substance – with disillusionment and ultimate failure inevitable.

Internal auditors in industry and government can and should serve the catalytic role. Surely there could be no better individual or chapter project than adopting a state or local government (or agency) and nurturing the internal audit function to successful fruition there. In what better way can a professional internal auditor pay his civic rent?